I'll Sleep

CW00740174

ADAM WORGAN

I'll Sleep When I Die

Matador
9 De Montfort Mews
Leicester LE1 7FW, UK
Tel: (+44) 116 255 9311
Email: books@troubador.co.uk
Web: www.troubador.co.uk

ISBN 1 904744 43 5

Typesetting: Troubador Publishing Ltd, Leicester, UK
Printed and bound by The Cromwell Press Ltd, Trowbridge, Wilts, UK

Matador is an imprint of Troubador Publishing Ltd

CONTENTS

INTRODUCTION

Time is the coin of your life.
It is the only coin you have, and only you can
determine how it will be spent.
Be careful lest you let other people spend it for you.
Carl Sandburg (1878–1967)

This book is a journey, a collaborative process, and if we are to help each other then we must start at the beginning and work forwards. I will be challenging you to review your current working practices to see where you are today, and in that way, when you come into contact with the concepts that will be explained in this book, you will soon realize just how much they can add to your own systems. We will work on how to plan your life; the benefits of establishing such a plan and the pitfalls that may need to be avoided. I will take you through practical ways of getting things done in a more efficient manner than you may now be achieving or even think possible. And once we have an idea of your own programme, we can then consider the most appropriate ways of improving it to start getting the results we want.

To this end, it will be worthwhile taking the time to not only read this book, but to take action on the points as they are raised. In this way, your learning and motivation will be reinforced, and it will help you to establish a system or improve the underlying problems with your present practices. This book is therefore designed to be read and re-read, moving from section to section and reviewed, as many times as is necessary, as we progress through the material.

We then need to look at how to progress these time planning skills so that you can develop your own ways of adaptation and improve and personalise the work that we start together. To do this, I will again be asking you to look at your thoughts about time and time management and, as the impetus is given to you to move you forward with the practical advice and tips from this book, you will quickly see that the process is very easy to master. The results will be obtained virtually straight away. We then need to look at the end result – a system that works for you; one that fits your own time patterns and also allows you the time to do all of the things that we dream about. We shall also look at how everything that we do will add or detract from the systems we develop, from our diet and drinking patterns to when we drink and eat, as well as our physical fitness and mental well-being. The benefits of this book will be limited if you do not have the strength to achieve the things that we want out of life.

As you will see, if all we want is more time to be out on the razz or more time in bed – as you do not like to be out of it – then you may as well stop reading now. This book is to help you achieve great things. It is not about helping someone, as I was once asked to do, show the appearance of looking as though they were productive and on top of things, their objective being that they did not have to do much as they would have all the other suckers doing their work for them! This is a book about helping you to achieve great things.

We will shortly meet and learn how to deal with:

1.   The Time Terrorist
2.   The Time Bandit
3.   The Time Assassin
4.   The Time Vandals
5.   Time Lord

I have some very tried and tested systems for the drawing up and monitoring of plans. As these represent the linchpin on which this concept is built upon, we will take great time and trouble to get this across to you and as often as possible so that it sticks in your mind. People ask me how to achieve a balance between their life and their work when they have so many problems to be resolved. And yet, the biggest problem we face today is our lack of control over our lives or at least that is what we have come to think of as the problem. Nonetheless, we do face ever-greater problems with travel and this is the overriding factor that people get so worked up about.

These problems have been building for many years, and they seem to be accelerating, and we're all powerless to bring about some improvement. Combined with an ineffective system of government and the widespread disenchantment and disengagement of the population, we are fed a diet of soap operas and mind-numbing programmes full of those without talent, people just looking for an easy way to make money and be famous, as if that is all that matters.

As you are reading this book, then you will have something inside you that is not fully cynical or jaded with life and that you are prepared to experience the satisfaction that comes from trying to do something about it.

We face a long struggle if we are going to look to central government to get things right for us, or for everyone else to stop using our roads when we do – surely they should all know how important our journeys are! We now have bus lanes that are designed to speed us past all the traffic. Unfortunately, if we are not working where the buses go, then they are of no use to us. If we do travel by public transport, there is often so little room that by the time we get to work we are not in the best frame of mind to excel at whatever it is we are doing. So, what do we do?

We can look at this whole issue in more detail especially if you travel for work or as a part of your day. Road rage is something of a new phenomenon, but it is more to do with letting off steam than problems we experience as part of the journey. If you have seen the film with Michael Douglas titled *Falling Down* you will know that we have a meek and mild every day person who becomes stuck in a traffic jam, his air conditioning is not working, the traffic build-up increases and he starts to get caught up in all of the other things that are going wrong in his life, which then impacts on his view of society. He gets out of the car, leaves it in the middle of the traffic and walks off. This, as you might well imagine, is when the real trouble starts. He queues up at a fast food outlet and orders a breakfast meal only to be told that it is now 11:01am and they stop preparing breakfast at 11:00am. He tries to remonstrate with the young boy behind the counter who is adamant. It is at this point that the problems of our protagonist really begin escalating out of control, and all because of one minute. It seems crazy; it is crazy, but that is how life can be. For the sake of just sixty seconds, people can lose all their bearings in reality. These are the TIME TERRORISTS.

To varying degrees, this is a scenario that most of us can generally relate to and it highlights an interesting fact that once we are inside the safety of our own cars, a strange sort of ambivalence can take over. On the one hand, we are aware of having less control in our lives (being on the road), and yet on the other hand, we can begin to feel invincible (the car is our safety shield). Should tensions build to flaring point, we can vent them with both barrels on the object of our rage to make ourselves feel better because there is a very great chance that we will never see this person ever again – added to which, they are outside our vehicle and our aggression cannot get us into trouble. The risk, however, is that some people continue to get just this bit braver each time such tensions overtake them, to the point that one day they find themselves in real trouble and outside the car, totally vulnerable and about to stand toe to toe with a stranger. As we all know only too well from the tragic headlines, such forays can end up being a last journey.

I was once given the finger by an old woman, and I was so shocked it took me all day to get it out of my head as to how it was possible for some little old lady to get so wound up with life that a purely inadvertent action by a stranger in a car could evoke such a fierce and – or, so I would have thought – out of character reaction. It is such a small thing, but our life is shaped these days by our reliance on time to the extent that it seems absolutely nothing should stand in its way. We have just been to war in the last year because one person decided that the time was up for someone else; that it was the best time to go to war after 10 years or so of not complying with rules. Although I am not against war in principle, I do believe that time should never be the arbiter of our actions.

Once we have no time to talk, to genuinely communicate, then we have lost it all. We need to always be aware that although the clock is ever ticking it is never our master; it must never control us. Therefore, the best way to describe this book is that it is based on the premise that we are to be the masters of time, wielding its great power with understanding and ease to achieve all of our goals in life.

Of course, the trouble with time is that you never know when yours is about to run out. If you were able to stop time or slow it down, what would you do with the time you now have? It is not the amount of time we all have but what we do with it that counts. Some people seem to be able to get so much done and never appear under any form of stress. Others are always running about like headless chickens, working longer and longer hours and going around in ever decreasing circles and achieving nothing.

In this book I will talk through practical ideas and new ways of thinking about how you can release yourself from the problems you may think you have. There are some other concepts that I think are best left to the end where we can talk about time travel and other new thinking on where we fit in.

If you look at some of the most powerful people on the planet they do not look after their own diaries; they have people telling them where they are, where there going, when to sit and what to say. I would not say that is where we need to get you to, but if we can get you back in control of your own life that will take away a lot of your current stress.

The first thing is to have a short trip back in time so we can see where you are today with your current thinking about time. Most of us are working with a mindset on the subject of time that will have been given to us by our parents, teachers, colleges and work environments.

Parents pass on a lot more than looks in their genes, and the way you think is part genetic and part nurture, i.e. taught. As soon as you are born you are shoehorned into a construct of time that is not natural and for which you are not ready; time to get up, time to go to sleep and time to eat. If you are lucky then the time environment in which you are being brought up in is the best and most suited for you. If you have children yourself, you will know all about the sleepless nights and feeding times when they will not eat, only to find a short time later they are asking for the very food they had earlier refused. You may also know that children can spend hours looking at simple things without boredom setting in. Yet something that looks very interesting to us can bore them in minutes. They will play a game of hide and seek for hours, long after you have become totally fed up with it. You may also know people or children who seem to move in slow motion, and no matter how much you shout, scold or pull your own hair out they are not going to go any faster and yet they get there in the end.

That is the thing with time; everyone's time moves at a different pace. The problems only occur when you have to interact with the rest of the world and other people's time. This was never a problem until you come up against Greenwich Mean Time (GMT). When it comes to time, this is where stress starts and finishes, and this is by no means to be construed as an attack on this great institution.

By the time you reach about four or five years of age you have a good handle on time, or so you think. If you never had problems with time in your own home, you can be sure that you will in school. This is where any free thinking ideas you may have about time are going to get squashed. You are now being taught to fit in with some basic time principles. You have to learn how to tell the time and to stop day-dreaming (or if you take on the principles in Chapter 1 then this is the most productive time you will ever spend). Schools think that they teach you how to be better citizens and how to read and write. Although they are very good at this, they are not very good at teaching creativity. This is not their speciality, as most people now going into teaching are not particularly spontaneous by nature. Again, this is not a slur on this fine body of people.

The bell tells you when to start working, when to play, what you have to think about and for how long for. Now you may not be a mathematician at 10 a.m. but you may be at 4p.m. Schools do not take this into account, and consequently all of your life is a time compromise. So this is why we are now looking for some answers to the questions that you are asking. The good thing is you already know the answers, though possibly you do not know the questions to ask. We are now at the point in our lives, normally about eight years of age when the next curved ball comes at us; the test with a time limit. Not only do they want you to recall things you learnt twelve months earlier but also they tell you how long you have to do it in. This is the origin of a lot of our problems with time. Your brain needs to be trained to be fast and to think about and then recall the right answers when you need them.

Have you ever heard some music on the radio and instantly known all of the words even if you had not previously heard it for years?

Or you cannot think of who sang it and then in the middle of the night, out comes the answer, even if you can't remember why you wanted to know it. This is how the mind really works. It has no thoughts about GMT; it works at its own time. If you can bend time so that the workings of your own mind and GMT fit together, then harmony can be the result.

While we dip in and out of it mentally, time is constant. If you want to achieve control of you're life and keep everything going, then you need to set time objectives.

The primary focus is a where you want to be and you can work towards that objective with the help of this book.

If we are to believe we can make changes in our lives and have more time available, we must remember that it only works if you have a goal for that extra time. If you do not, then why go to the trouble of making a change at all as things will soon revert to the way they once were, with an even bleaker view of it in the future.

Bringing time scales and time management into your daily life will take time itself and, at first, can seem self-defeating. However, as with any investment, if you go into it with the risks and rewards properly and fully explained, then you will realise it as an investment rather than a payment.

ONE

TIME ON MY MIND

If one advances confidently in the direction of his dreams,
and endeavours to live the life which he has imagined he will
meet with success unexpected in common hours.
Henry David Thoreau

Once we have a grip on time, then we just need to spend a chapter giving you some understanding of how you think of time, and why. The possibility of not doing anything, for half an hour per day, just in quiet contemplation – and the benefits to time management. If I had my way I would teach all children how to sit and daydream as part of the schools curriculum.

Time is like sand running through your fingers – if you try to keep your hands closed then you are not going to be able to hold other things. Sometimes time management is about letting go of things, and thus letting go of the stress related to it to as well.

WHAT ARE WE GOING TO DO WITH HIM?

"What are we going to do with him?" they said, looking at a small boy sitting in the corner. There was nothing particularly different about him; kind of average height for his age and no real problems with his behaviour. But they could not teach him so they just let him sit there, wrapped in his own world, looking out the window dream-

1

ing dreams of swimming with dolphins or flying with the birds – free and easy. Who had the problem is a question rather like Buddha's gift.

Who has the problem? The boy is happy with his lot. On the other hand, the teachers are getting concerned for he is eight years old and he cannot read yet – he has a life expectancy of around 80 to 90 years, with less than 10% of his life gone. They focused on the problem from their own perspective. They were there to teach, and they were failing. As I have already touched on, schools are only happy when things are going to the expected norm – if this is not achieved you are an under-performer.

"What are we going to do with him?" They talk to his parents; he had been to five different schools in a short space of time as his parents were in the Royal Air Force – none of these schools could do anything with him. All they did was let him sit in the corner and dream; not the best way of going forward, just to let him sit there, but what can they do with him? The problem was one of time, as his time zone was out of sync with the rest of his class and he could not read as well as the others. As some people develop physically slower than others, so we develop the ability to grasp scholastic learning at different speeds, yet we may have great abilities that others may never have at a young age.

He was, however, very bright, good at joining in play activities, good at artistic things, always drawing with flare and using lots of colours, and he was always able to describe his efforts with great enthusiasm. It was not until a very bright teacher spent time in the boy's own time zone that he was diagnosed with dyslexia. Within six months he was reading at the same level as his classmates. He was very happy with his new-found skills, and the teachers were happy that he now fitted in to their module, and that he was now able to come up to speed with the rest of the class.

It was then that they began to stifle his creativity and bring him up to speed with the rest of the class – and stop that terrible daydreaming. (This Boy was me.)

Einstein as a boy was labelled with low intelligence, a daydreamer, by his teachers, but he turned out to be okay. The point of this story is that if we are to truly excel in our lives, we must daydream. It is the way the brain gets its energy, and it is the only way of helping you to maintain high levels of focused thinking. Time management is all about being happy with your own abilities, to comprehend what task is best suited to be achieved at what time and in which order.

It is very important you understand that all great things happen twice, once in the mind then in reality. All great inventions were first a thought and then someone brought them into the real world. It is therefore imperative that we spend time with our own thoughts so that we can become the shapers of time, and the ones that bring order to chaos. The problem for most people is that this basic part of time planning is the most difficult. They feel guilty that they are taking time to just sit and think when there is so much that needs to be achieved. But if we truly believe that we are here at this moment in time, looking for the answers to the question of how to achieve more with less stress, then how can this be? Spending time doing nothing might seem like an oxymoron, but it is one of the best kept secrets in the world. Doing less is going to help you achieve more in the time you have left.

Do we use our own abilities to plan in our minds first before committing things to paper first? What we need to do is dedicate time to relax – sit in a room or outside where you find it peaceful and where you know you will not be disturbed for about half an hour. At the start the optimum is two sessions of about 15 minutes per working day. If you can achieve this, then you will find you will feel so much more able to cope with life and problems with time. You may even get to the stage of having so much free time on your hands that you become bored. That is when you have to stop yourself getting involved with things just to fill your time. You will see this when we cover the delegation of tasks, not spending time doing the things that you have delegated. Trust me – at first you will!

So are you seated in that quiet spot? Or perhaps not if you are saying "hang on a minute – first, where do I find the time?" Well, what time do you get up at present? If you think about it, most people have trouble with sleep, and this is largely down to bad habits such as eating late at night and too much coffee or tea, maybe even alcohol. Coffee and tea stop the brain from starting properly when low levels of their dominate chemicals are present, so we spend all day topping them up, then at night we find it hard to drop off as these chemicals are present aplenty – we then find it hard to switch off.

For most people, though, it is their brain that has not switched off. So you lie there in the dark trying to sleep, and the brain thinks "Ah! Got them to myself now, they have not listened to me all day – now I'll tell them all the things they didn't get done today, or how bad they were to shout at the children. I must tell them they spent money today that they don't have, or that they ate that cake and don't they know they are on a diet?" As we know, we all talk to ourselves throughout the day, but we are so busy that we ignore it – to our peril. So, the first step in this process is to take the time out to listen to our own brain, and allow it to help us with our problems.

We then may start a new cycle by drinking a glass of wine at night to help us relax, which it may well do. Unfortunately, it may make us drowsy, but studies have shown that it may also stop us from reaching deep sleep states needed to make us feel refreshed in the mornings. So what do you do as you struggle to wake up? You have a cup of coffee or tea, and we start the cycle all over again. This cycle will destroy any real ability to master time, and the ability to truly think about why we are looking for more time to do the same things we are already doing. Being fully aware of the true reasons why we are unable to manage our time effectively is as much about new techniques of time planning as it is about discovering the real you, your own time cycle, and the outside effects other things have on it.

So the ability to be brutally honest to ourselves is the main reason why I believe we need to spend time in quite contemplation and future planning. The quiet time you spend with yourself is critical for time planning, as many of the techniques we shall look at later in this book need this time to apply time planning tools, task lists and focus tools.

Empty our minds as much as possible and have a note pad and a pencil, because some of your best ideas will come and go in this short space of time. Recording them will be relevant later when we introduce you to next day-time planing. Once we have our free time to sit and think, we become very protective of it. I find that for me, first thing in the morning when walking the dogs, and last thing at night when I am just settling things in my office, is the most productive time for me. A proposed 30 minutes of time out of every 1440 in a day is all I am are suggesting – not a great amount of time in the grand scheme of things, yet probably the best 30 minutes of the day for relieving future stress around time planning.

Once in a quiet place we need to just let our minds wander for the first few seconds, even in the first few minutes. Once it has settled down, we can start to plan some of the tasks we shall need to plan for what we are going to do today, and what it is we hope to get out of the day. Once we have the practicalities of the day out of the way, then we need to build the big dreams. Over time we will get great amounts of time planning ideas from this time, which in turn will give us more time to spend planning. It becomes a self-perpetuating time planning tool, taking time but giving time back in ideas to overcome problems and situations. By writing these down and reviewing them on a regular basis, we can start to plan our long-term strategies for developing our own time management programme that is particular to our own lives and work needs.

This book is about time control. However, it is important we have a good understanding of how our own mind works so as to maximise the benefits of our quiet time so it becomes our productivity engine.

The human mind is indeed a wondrous and complex thing, but it is also very simple in its operation. It has two basic parts: the conscious – the part that we are able to work with – tells us what we are doing and how to do it; when we are going to write a letter to a loved one, it is the bit that gets pen to paper. It also acts as a judge in deciding *what we like, what we don't like and whether we are going here, there or nowhere.*

It very closely resembles the RAM drive on a computer, in that it deals with everything that is going on at a conscious level. If we are going to drive to the shops, it will tell us which turning to go down, when to stop and when to go. In its most brilliant state it can have a specificity of focus that is quite singular in terms of what it can do. With training it can be programmed to do very complex things, and can even get us to overcome great pain. However, like an iceberg, the top end can be seen, but the largest part is hidden.

The real powerhouse is the subconscious mind, which is a very efficient storeroom. It has no thought processes, but it keeps a record of everything that happens. It records events in your life that you have not remembered in a conscious state. It is said that your subconscious will have remembered every number plate that you were not conscious of seeing. It makes no judgement, yet it has awesome power to achieve the greatest of dreams.

Good thoughts will be kept self-limiting; bad thoughts will be kept like soil, where they can grow weeds or beautiful flowers.

Have you ever experienced the situation where you hear a song on the radio and you wonder who sang it? No matter how much you think about it consciously, you cannot recall who it was. You tell yourself that you can't remember, so your mind – the subconscious – says, okay, you are right (it makes no judgement, you are right; you cannot remember the name of the singer). The subconscious mind thinks that's it, and nothing else happens. However, what usually happens is that you end up with this mental statement that "it will come to me in a minute." Off we then go, after the next thing that our conscious mind has to deal with; dinner or the phone call that needs to be made. Later on that day, or even in the middle of the night, the subconscious mind says "you have mail", and up pops the singer's name! At the same time, it brings up a visual image and a snippet of the song, as well as memories of anyone linked to that part of your life and to whom the song is related in your mind.

As the subconscious mind cannot make decisions, it follows directions from the conscious mind. Imagine a man driving one of those huge earth moving machines, knowing that for as long as he is paying attention it is safe, and so is everyone close by. But if he gets down from the machine and leaves it to run on its own, then even at a slow idle it can do a huge amount of damage. In your early life you don't have the skills to run your subconscious, so others programme it, and many of us will carry self-limiting beliefs that are given to us in those early years.

Nowadays the world is full of people who are screwed up by that earlier programming, no matter how well intentioned the givers of that information may have been. People will have hang-ups about their appearance from off-the-cuff comments that a parent, grandparent or even a teacher might have made. From that input into the conscious mind, it is then fed into the subconscious. Every time it gets to the subconscious mind it grows, and if it gets there a few times the subconscious will try to obtain corroboration – evidence to back up the information received from the conscious.

What I mean by this is that every time your conscious mind says something, your subconscious mind starts working on it subliminally, in the background if you like, and usually ends up achieving its objective.

So every time you say to yourself, "I am going to be late for this appointment", or "I am always late for appointments", then your subconscious mind says "Okay", and begins to reinforce the messages you are sending it—and guess what... you develop a chronic problem with being late! The same will happen to you if, over a period of time, you are constantly told as a child to "Hurry up, you're going to be late, or you're so slow... come on, get a move on, you're going to make me late". You get conditioned to waiting for others to hurry us up, and with out this input we can even grind to a halt, unable to move without a 'gee-up' from others.

This can become a very obvious characteristic; you know the one in the office– there's always one – who is always late, and the running joke is "Where is so and so? You don't think that they will be on time, do you? Come on, let's get going with out them." These people are some of the rudest in the world, and should be avoided at all costs, and we know them as the TIME TERORISTS. They are always running out of time, or keeping you waiting; stealing time from everyone they come in contact with. Never give your time away to such people. *It is your time and they do not have the authority to take it from you.* There are practical tips on how to deal with people like this later.

We can, as with most things in life, change the input and receive a different result (like a computer).

You have no doubt heard the saying "Only a fool expects to get different results by doing the same things" (if we do what we have always done we will always get what we have always got). Sounds pretty simple, yet many people have this as their core philosophy in life.

To shake ourselves out of these self-limiting results is so important if we are going to change our time planning results. The best way to change things, as we already know, is in the mind first, then translate this into reality. The use of positive time affirmations is the easiest way of achieving this. These are good if used during the quiet times we set aside to relax in as an opening to bring relaxation to the time.

TWO

THINKING POSITIVELY

Use positive time affirmations:

- I have a very efficient time management system

- I am always on time for appointments

- My diary is always set out in a practical manner

- Time is important to me, and I give others time respect

- Only I have the right to decide what time I have to do things in

- I spend 30 minutes every day in quiet contemplation and planning for my tomorrows

- I love life and it loves me as I have time respect for others and myself

THREE

WHERE DID THE TIME GO?

This is an introduction to where our time goes in supporting others in their dismally ill-timed worlds – and which may even be us at present – read on...

People with no time management skills are generally easy to deal with, as they will be in awe at your skill with time control and, generally, with some training, will become very compliant to your requests, turning into your very best aide in helping with tasks that need doing. Give the work to them with a very short time limit. As they are in chaos, at first they will generally do it, but with some complaining. However, lots of praise from you is something they will not get from elsewhere and, over a short period of time, they can become quite good at working with your system so there is no contest when meetings are being arranged.

People who are late are to be avoided at all costs. As with most such people, it is only when they have to interact with us that the problems begin. If they need to come to your meetings, give them the job of receptionist or greeting attendees. Alternatively, arrange a one-to-one meeting with them first – if they are late it has given you time to set up; if they turn up, then they can help you. Force them to comply with your time regime, not the other way around.

People with elaborate time management systems spend so much time with two diaries or palm-tops that always seam to have flat batteries, and need to update every five minutes with the main diary on the PC. These people never seem to allow time for problems or time for a break, or even to walk from one side of the office to the other, so they are generally late or only just on time – looking very efficient for busy people who frequently never get anything done. They are generally so very technical about time that they always have to possess the latest timesaving gadget. They then spend days learning how to use the item, only to discard it when they realise they are no better off time-wise than before. The other people are the Colombo's of this world, producing notes from themselves to themselves about things; always looking for the things they filed away in the special system that nobody can fathom when our friend is not there.

Incompetent people are reminders of what used to be said of these people in the 'old days', and known as the *Peter Principle*. This principle states that people rise in an organisation to the level of their incompetence to do the job, then get sacked, demoted or moved sideways and given a fancy title. Whichever way you look at it, these people will suck you into their world and tie up your time while you do your job and theirs, because you are either their boss or they yours... or because you feel sorry for them. They will grow more and more reliant on your time if you are not careful. If possible, avoid them, or help to teach them to either do the job themselves or pass the task on to someone else. I know this may sound difficult, but remember – we are here to help *you* get control of your time so that you feel more in control and less stressed.

Meetings of any sort are where *minutes are taken and hours are lost.* The first thing is the start time. Is it 10.00a.m. for a 10.30a.m. start, and if so, what does that mean? Invariably, people will be late and there will be those who will be trying to have a quick smoke just as you are about to start the meeting. It is much better to have the meeting start at 10.00a.m. on the nose (or whatever time) – make it known that you are not tolerating lateness as it is disrespectful to others, and it is other people's time they are stealing. To set this in context, if you have 10 people in a room and the meeting starts 10 minutes late, then that's about the same as burning £50 of the company's money. It may not seem a lot, but think how many meetings may be happening in a large company throughout the day – over a year that is a vast waste of money at a time when many company's are trying to reduce costs.

Get five or six small items out of the way quickly, then have a five-minute coffee break after an hour. Even better, don't have coffee, just water. Fresh water is still the best; that way only comfort breaks will be needed (and if you're meeting in a hotel it will also be cheaper!).

Time the meeting by the minutes allocated to each agenda item, e.g.

- Start at 10.00
- Introductions 5 mins
- John Smith reorders problems—10 mins
- Harry Ryder the small chain development—20 mins
- Marry Stevens's design of the widget—25 mins

You can see this makes timing easy to work with, and helps people time their part. They also know how much work they are expected to put in for their reporting segment or talk.

It also pays to put in the type of thing they are expected to contribute, and whether it will be a report or if they will be using media such as PowerPoint™ or flipcharts. If reports are technical, if possible have these distributed prior to the meeting so that everyone has the chance to peruse them and make comments before the meeting. This avoids the need for prolonged discussion while the presentation is underway.

If people are going to use computer technology, such as laptop presentations, have them emailed to you before the meeting so their programme can be set up on one laptop that you will know works with the projector, thus reducing handover time between presenters. You are also able to set out the sections and put them in order – and also have a look prior to the meeting, thus being forewarned.

By using time allocation rather than a start or finish time per segment, it is easy to have a meeting that starts early or late. This also means that people are able to plan things in advance of the meeting, and are therefore more in control of their own time. Meetings must have a start time and an end time. Unless everyone is in agreement that it should continue, a meeting must end on time even if all the items have not been finalised.

Always have timing in mind when you set a meeting's agenda, but don't overdo it. If the agenda is too busy it may get people thinking that the objective of the meeting is to skim over things too lightly, and it may seem there is little point in holding the meeting. Every meeting is important if it achieves its objectives, but these must be established at the outset so that people are under no illusion as to why they are there. If meetings are being held away from the office, in a hotel for example, then start them early and finish them late, as this is the only reason to hold them outside the office environment. If things go wrong at an out-of-office location, it can waste valuable time trying to get the information required for the meeting.

The time keeping of the meeting is very important, so whenever possible, ask someone to look after the timing for you. What the time-keeper says goes, as this is crucial to keep the meeting moving along. In this way people will not get overtired or bored.

People will still drift in and out of the meeting mentally, so if it is a long meeting, it is important to allow controlled interjections at the discretion of the chair, and invite comments from attendees so that they maintain a participatory involvement with the various agenda items.

Any Other Business meetings segments are also to be avoided. Never have this session at meetings as it just ends up taking over, and it can last longer than the main meeting. You will see people sit in a meeting for hours and say nothing, then come to life when Any Other Business comes up to talk about smelly toilets or the wrong coloured envelopes that this or that department are using.

Agendas. Every meeting, no matter how short, must have a written agenda. If you are in charge of the agenda, make sure that whenever possible, attendees are asked to complete a list of things to be discussed at the forthcoming meeting. You will then have everyone's own agenda, and you can choose to fit in the things that are relevant. Participants are then tasked to present on that item, and control that part of the given timing for that section of the meeting. If, at the end of the allotted time, this item is not fully resolved, you can schedule more time outside the meeting to finalise the matter and get it resolved, with the outcome to be reported back at the next meeting. Alternatively, in agreement with all parties to carry on with discussion, try and get back on track later after a sorting out break. If possible, the agenda should be circulated a few days before the meeting so that everyone knows what is going to be covered. Remember, if it is not on the agenda, then it is not in the meeting, unless everyone including you agrees.

If you're attending a meeting then try to get the agenda a few days before, as this forces people to become more organised around you, giving you more control over your own diary. If there is something on the agenda that you would like to talk about, ask the person who is in charge as soon as possible if you can have an opportunity to talk about that subject. If there are topics for the meeting that will not involve you, then try to turn up earlier and ask to be excused while these points are discussed. I would not advocate you and everyone else coming and going from the meeting every 10 minuets or so, but if it is an all day meeting, then you may not be needed, for example, until the afternoon.

Mobile Phones are a fascinating subject in meetings as you will no doubt be accustomed to the general start to most meetings. In the case of a fire, follow me out this way; turn off mobiles – £10 for the first one to go off. The meeting starts, and most people have turned them to silent, on the desk in front of them. They will inevitably look to see who is calling as it lights up. The only way to deal with this is:

1.   Request that THEY ARE SWITCHED OFF AND OUT OF SIGHT.

2.   Best if possible put in a bin and left under your control until the end of the day.

3.   Passed to reception or someone outside the meeting if there is a urgent need, such as an expected birth, and a call is expected any day. If this is the case, should someone that will more than likely spend most of the meeting thinking about that than the meeting be at a meeting of importance? Remember, all meetings are important.

4.   Unless it is business relating to the meeting or company, request that people do not use mobiles during breaks in the meeting.

FOUR

HOW DO YOU EAT AN ELEPHANT?

Time management is all about thinking in segments – allocating tasks to fit into the time that is available. This means we must be very *flexible* and *rigid* at the same time:

- *Flexible* enough to move tasks about the day to accommodate a moving work environment.
- *Rigid* enough so as not to be put off an unpleasant task or allowing others to highjack your day, as discussed in the chapters on TIME TERRORISTS.

This system of time management is very easy to use, and makes no reference to the type of task, but rather the type of time and when to carry out the task. If you are fully in control of your own life, then your stress levels are lower, giving you greater energy to complete the task you want to achieve.

If we think of time as fluid rather than rigid, we can also consider energy in the same way. There is an unlimited supply of energy that is constantly and freely available to us, but we just need to know how to tap into it. This is very important, and is a key factor in your being happy to move from where you are today to where you wish to be.

TIP

Small Tasks are better scheduled for low energy level times, as completed tasks give us a physical and, more importantly, a mental boost of energy.

TIME TASKS

- Small filing jobs, e.g. desk tidying
- Report writing
- Meetings
- Travelling
- Phone calls
- Job specific tasks
- Down time awaiting for others to do their job before you can complete yours
- Post including emails (reading and sending)

There are probably many others that you can relate to your own job and life situation, but let's look at some other evidence before tackling them one at a time.

As with all of these things, you have to believe it to see it. If you are always looking for proof first, then many things in life will evade you – that is just the way it is. There is only 5% or less of the total population of the world who will achieve great wealth or notoriety, but that does not mean that all of the world's truly great riches are not always available to you. This is the same with time, as there are some basic principals that, once mastered, will be with you for life. No mater what your current position or outlook, they can make a difference.

Life is there; we all have one. Let's not have it go to waste by being worried about taking a risk or two – open your mind to the riches available to you.

Moving forward from this, it is very important that we get to grips

---

TIP
The World is there for the risk takers

with these things earlier rather than later. I have met people who were dead at 20, and it will take the next 40–50 years for their bodies to catch up. If you listen to these negative people, then life will stay the same and pass you by. One thing is for sure: no-one will ever be able to get back the time lost or wasted. Dreaming of the past and believing you can get it back and change it will always be a disaster.

TIPS

You can only step in a running stream once

Achieving congruency in life is very important

Being in the moment sounds a very easy thing to say, but to truly be in the moment takes a great deal of skill and can never be achieved fully without practice and patience

---

OVER CONCENTRATING ON ONE TASK TO THE DETRIMENT OF OTHERS

Nature is very clever at stopping us from doing things. In focusing too long and too intently, you will eventually end up with nothing. Take, for example, the way in which our eyes work.

Eyes are only working when they are constantly moving about, so eyes move and lids blink and you are able to see the big picture. On the other hand, if you stare at an object for a long time you lose sight of the big picture, and your view begins to contract and become smaller. Things start to close in and we develop tunnel vision. If we continue to stare at the object things will continue to close in until eventually everything disappears, and there is only blackness. Only a blink will bring it all back. So a blink, a reality check, is essential from time to time as we look at the bigger picture in order to sustain greater focus and increased intensity for longer and more prolonged periods of time.

With many seemingly dysfunctional families and the break up of a vast number of marriages, people blame a lack of control and time as the number one failure in many relationships. There is the father thinking his only task is to earn money and unwittingly letting his family down by not being there when they need him. One day he wakes up to find his children will despise him, and his wife no longer loves him. This happens more often than you might think is possible.

When I spend time with people in this position it takes a little while for them to take a good, objective look at themselves before we can move forward. As with all problems, self-actualisation and realisation are important and integral features of time management. Only when we can take hold of this concept and truly understand it will things start to become clear, so that we can move our lives forward.

Only then will all the other things we need to work on be achieved. Given that we take on more and more in our lives, being able to assimilate things that are important and fit them into our big picture, so we can move forward is always going to be of great importance. There are some days when time-related issues are very hard to define, as what is an issue for you may not be an issue for me, and vice versa.

So how do we eat an elephant BIT BY BIT – how do we start to get our lives back BIT BY BIT? The following will start to make some headway into the seemingly crisis hit world in which we spend our lives.

FIVE

CRUNCH
THIS NEEDS TO BE DONE
YESTERDAY

One of the main areas people tell me about is that time just alludes them – they have all the best intentions of doing an outstanding job, but end up delivering a rushed piece of work that does the job, but only just, and gets you no extra recognition.

REPORT WRITING

To get a report out on time we sometimes dedicate a whole day or even a week to it, to the exclusion of all other things we would normally do. The first few minuets are okay, then other normal interruptions start. Yes, we may have decided to tell others we are not to be disturbed, unless it is vitally important. They will then bother you with everything while determining how large a problem has to be in order for you to be disturbed.

The following tips, if followed, will reduce the time it takes to complete the task by up to 50%, and the quality will probably be higher.

1. Work from home if possible (so long as office disturbances are not replaced by home-based ones).
2. Book into a separate office somewhere away from your normal work station.

3. Work from a local hotel – these are the best free office facilities available.
4. Delegate one person to cover all of your normal tasks, as if you were on holiday, and don't get involved with anything.
5. Have all of the information available to you before you start (this can be and should be a separate task in itself).
6. Set goals and agendas for the report, and how long you are going to spend on each area – don't over-elaborate.

DOWN-TIME WAITING FOR OTHERS

1. Always leave people to get on with their own jobs (standing chatting to the engineer next to the broken photocopier does not get the copier fixed any quicker – standing next to them with all of the copying you were about to do does not make them work any harder).
2. Have back-up tasks such as small filling jobs or phone calls ready for such a time.
3. Take an early break while others do their work.
4. Communication is a one-way process, so makes sure a delegated task is understood and timescales accepted and agreed at the start. Be specific as to how much detail you require and when it is to be returned. Always be practical – it may only take you a short time to do this, but the less competent helper may take a little longer.
5. Expect there to be down time and plan for it.

The other areas are covered through out this book.

TIMING IS EVERYTHING

So how do we deal with time in a practical way? The quick fix for most people is not to wear a watch during the week, and only if necessary should it be worn on the weekends. I realise this goes against most current thinking on time. Why would you wear a watch during the week and not at weekends? Let me explain the concept – you have your work life timed to the millisecond, and your own time, free and relaxed. This nevertheless causes you a great deal of stress, as you go 'cold turkey' every two days out of seven.

Slipping into a different time situation will generally make it more difficult to get back to work on Monday. This can lead to an increase in stress that is attributable to another 'new' lack of control element over our working lives when we get into the "I hate my job" mindset, which really can accelerate the downward spiral. Yet this was meant to alleviate the problem, not make it worse.

By turning things on their end and working watch-less, you get more done overall – and on the weekends as well, because you do not just spend them in bed in recovery mode.

When you stop wearing a watch you actually gain time. I am not advocating being late for everything and just drifting around hapless and lost, milling about not knowing what to do next. Some of our working lives are very rigid, and there is little time for us to move freely. You do not need to know what the time is, as someone will surely tell you when to do the next thing.

Most of you reading this book will find it is possible for you to have a great deal of control over your time, even total control, through planning your own diary, reappraising the top end of the organised world and acting on the clues that are available – looking for a different handle on aspects that have become habitual and unthinking.

Top politicians will have a team of people controlling their every move and running their diary; they only do what is needed when it is needed. They will be in meetings all day, and not necessarily know what they will be doing later on that day or week, or where it is or how they are going to get there, as this is all done for them. You do not see President Bush sitting there, looking at his watch, during a meeting thinking he should be at home. He is where he is until some one says, "Mr President, It is time to go."

Now I know it is highly unlikely the other people in that meeting will say "What! Part time today?" or "I have not finished yet; sit back down" but you get the gist. Rock stars on tour may not even know which country they are in, let alone the time of day or what is happening next. They just get driven, flown or carried from one place to another.

They say that Frank Sinatra would walk on stage, sing and walk off. He would not be there during the day moving the piano or setting up the lighting rig, so why do so many of us delegate a task only to watch the task being done, or redo it without involving the person to whom it was delegated? Masters of time are also master trainers and master of delegation. These are the most overlooked tasks, yet we perform them every day; doing the things that make us look busy even when we are not.

A BARE WRIST – LIVING WITH OUT A WATCH

1. Others are happy to remind you if you are going to be late – have others clock watch for you.

2. Set aside the time to complete a task and time it with a reminder clock, rather than keep looking at a time piece and working out when to stop.

3. Less time wasted stopping to look at our wrist also helps us give time respect in meetings (covered in Chapter 11).

4. Frees us from worry about being late, as all things can be

time allocated rather then have a start and must be finished by time.

5. Keeps us focused on the task at hand.

6. Stops us drawing out a task (they say if you have all day to do one thing it will take all day – if you have 20 minutes the same task will take you 20 minutes. Remember we are trying to gain time to do other things, possibly be at home with our familles, so don't spend a day doing a 20 minute task.

7. Your own internal clock will switch on and you will soon be able to judge a time span to within minutes, so you can remain focused throughout the meeting/ task.

8. Contract with others to remain time task-oriented, rather then time deadlocked.

9. Still keep meetings with start times and finish times, just section the time into segments rather than have separate start and finish times for each item.

10. Try not to swap the watch for all of the other time machines around (there is a list further on in the book).

SIX

THE MYTH OF LONG HOURS

"I must work longer hours to keep my job; it is expected of me." First, you need to understand we only need to work 20 hours per week to have the same standard of living as we had in the sixties. A 40-hour week will get us a modern life – anything over that is money in the bank. With most modern-thinking companies, it is more important that the work is done in a quick and timely manner rather than being worked on over an extended period of time. It would be silly to think that a 100-meter sprinter could maintain that pace for the length of a marathon. So if you are expected to work more then 10–12 hours per day, then you are going to burn out, and the company will have lost money on their investment – You!

It is therefore imperative that you look after yourself both physically and mentally, as both need exercise and rest. Physically it is very important that you have high levels of energy, and that means eating regularly throughout the day and drinking plenty of still water. Now I do not subscribe to the 20 gallons of spring water or whatever they say it should be. Water out of the tap will do you as much good, if not better than bottled water out of some well or spring. *Never drink coffee, tea or sugar-laden fizzy drinks, and never, never smoke.*

When I say no tea, I mean no tea, not even this herbal stuff they say is good for you. I challenge you if you can stop drinking any of this stuff for six months then try and drink it again – you will be shocked at how the body reacts to it. Remember, it takes 21 days to make or break a habit, and the only way to stop an addiction is cold turkey.

All of these things are as addictive as any other drug.

You just believe that they are okay, yet how many people say "I can't do anything until I have had at least two cups of coffee in the morning, and then it needs to be stronger and more of it to just be able to start off the day, and more and more to maintain it." Is this not the same as any drug – cocaine, crack? They all mess with your physical ability, and definitely screw up your mind. The simple test is if you would not give it to a four year old, then it is not likely to do you any good either.

Regular snacks throughout the day will keep your energy levels up. It is also important to find somewhere different to go to eat your lunch, meet with a friend, sit outside. If possible, go for a walk, read a book even if it is for only twenty minutes a day – you will see the difference in your ability to get work done in the afternoon. It is never a good idea to eat a big lunch, even if you have to have a lunch meeting. It is better to let others have the big heavy food, especially if you are in negotiations with them; while they are still digesting their meal, you can maintain your mental edge and get the good deals.

They say that breakfast is the most important meal of the day, and there are many thoughts on diet. The most important thing to remember is that part of the joy of eating is that it stimulates the mind in more ways than one. From the time management perspective, having the time to eat properly is again something we will achieve if we have a system to rely on and work with.

As food is fuel, our intake needs to be monitored. If you had a multi-million pound racehorse, would you keep it up all night smoking and drinking, feeding it on take-away or fast food, and then giving it only a few hours sleep, and then still expect it to win races the next day? I dare say you would not treat a £300 pound dog or even a £10 cat in this way.

Yet we have gained this 'work hard, play hard' thinking which, when you are 20 and feel invincible, may be okay. Yet over the years it will get to you, without you being able to do anything about it. It's then too late. So food is as important to time management as the diary itself. Designating time to eat with your family is a very important thing to do, yet beating yourself up over it because you are stuck in traffic is of no use either.

If you are able to establish a working pattern that is in line with your own body's rhythm, you can maintain a very high level of work for extended periods of time. This should negate the long work hours ethic that still pervades in some work environments. If you have to travel during the course of your regular working routine, then this is one of the easiest ways in your day to either lose time or make great use of time.

If you ask someone in the office how long it will take to get to the other side of town, the answer that usually follows is something like this:

You How long do you think it will take me to get over to Happy Street?
Office helpful person Oh about 20 minuets.

You Oh that's okay. I have 30 minuets before I have to leave, and I will have time to park – thanks.

Office helpful person Oh I didn't know you meant now! It will take you about 50 minutes at this time of day. I can do it in 20 minuets on the way back from here on a late shift at about 10p.m. But I think you're going to be late – should have asked earlier.

We should also plan our journeys with great thought. It is better to leave early and take some easy tasks with us to do in the car when we get there if we are early. This also means that if you are collared in the office as you are going, you still have time to get there.

Travelling Time end game
- Easy tasks
- Reading journals to keep up to date
- Making phone calls
- Booking appointments
- Updating task lists
- Listening to motivational tapes
- Reading up on forthcoming appointment
- Confirming later appointments
- Free thinking time for future planning
- Rehearsal of scripts.

As you can see, there is a varity of tasks that can be achieved in the car when waiting to go into a call. You can also go in early if you think the other person will see you early.

GOLDEN RULE OF TIME MANAGEMENT

If you are the one who is doing the travelling, then you are using the other person's time and they are in Control.

Whenever possible, make people come to you or meet halfway. The important thing is if you are going to someone else, then they are in control, so don't block out the rest of the day unless they say so. Agree beforehand how long you have – if they are a TIME LORD expect them to stick to it.

SEVEN

TIME TERRORISTS

Don't say you don't have enough time.
You have exactly the same number of hours per day that
were given to Helen Keller, Pasteur, Michelangelo,
Mother Teresa, Leonardo da Vinci, Thomas Jefferson,
and Albert Einstein.
H. Jackson Brown

As we know, TIME TERRORISTS come in all shapes and sizes. At first, some will be flattering and will not seem like a problem, but if it is not on your radar, then it will divert you from the task at hand. Below is a list of classic time terrorists:

- People with no time management skills*
- Late people*
- 'Any Other Business' sessions at the end of meetings. Never have them (the biggest thing to remember about meetings is that "they are where minutes are taken and hours are lost")*
- People with elaborate time management systems*
- Incompetent people*
- Meetings of any sort*
- The "can you come over and give us a talk about XYZ at our meeting?"*
- The "I have been having a problem with this; can you cast your eye over it as I need to hand it in, in ten minutes."

- No shows or, if you are being positive, me shows.
- People with too much time on their hands.*
- The coffee cup brigade.*
- 'Neg heads' who just have to tell you how bad things are.'*
- Queues that you do not have to be in.*
- E-mails that come in throughout the day (in the 'old days' you would have read your post once per day).
- Traffic jams (always have a good book or tape for just that occasion).
- Friends and family.
- Mobile phones.
- Mobile phone text messages.
- You can add to the list, otherwise the list will become one.

These are all covered in other chapters in the book, and are mentioned more than once

As we know, terrorists rarely show up when you are ready for them. Instead, it is the car bomb or sniper attack.

Time is relative, and lots of very high level books have been written on the subject. What we are looking at is getting others to work with you, so that the people with whom you are interacting value your time. Look at this statement and think of the people you know to whom it applies. Yes, these are the time terrorists; never in full view, but always skulking in the background and then, bang, without warning off goes their bomb!

Your lack of planning does not constitute an emergency on my part

It is their lack of planning that gets you if you are not on your guard.

They will have hang ups from the past, but time has deadened their senses to the point where they no longer know what they are against, just they are against it.

If this is how they treat you, then it is as much to do with how they view your time as to how they wiew their own. In the beginning, time terrorists will react with scepticism and will challenge your new time-bending skills. They will try to stop your progress to the land of easy planning and extra time. The time terrorist has fundamental-ism on his side.

They say that:

You will need to stand for something or you will fall for everything

It is the same for the time terrorist, many of whom are simply led by a lack of willingness to conform to basic work ethic. This leads them to becoming envious of your developing skills. They will try and hijack your time or the time of others who you have asked to assist you. As terrorists, this is their preferred method – slowly working on the younger people who will be working on tasks for you.

This is especially relevant if you are part of a development team and they are on the outside looking in. They will move about the office looking for the person with time-critical research on which others are dependent, and in they go.

Usually this involves offers of coffee or tea, such as "I was just off down to the coffee machine; like one?" This may seem like a nice offer, but this is what happens next: "Here's your coffee." "Thanks." This will be followed by "What are you working on?" "Is it for that plonker xx? I heard he is losing the plot over this." Followed by "So and so (they will always involve others) said you were all under a lot of strain to get this lot finished by the end of the week; it seems like you are going to be here all night – I hope you brought your pyjamas." And, "Did you see the game last night? I can't believe they played xx out on the right wing. If I were you I would tell him where to stick his special project." And to complete the friendly hijack, "Are you coming down the pub at lunchtime?"

As you can see, these people ask just a few questions when they know you are not really listening, but it is in there for later, when you begin to think "Why am I the last one still here working. 'Fred' does seem to have a point." To the time terrorist who is working this line, it is only a slogan or chant, maybe even a call to rally, but the big bombs will come and, if you're not prepared, younger team members can be blown away from the task for days, and valuable time on projects can be lost.

Most of the time, the time terrorist is only a distraction, but key critical areas of planning can grind to a halt when a team member is caught up in their actions. Terrorists may not stop you from getting the job done, but their ability to get in the way of complex time management systems should never be underestimated.

They do not always operate on their own. In a large company they can infiltrate the entire organisation and try to bring it to its knees. I have nothing against unions, but this is one of their favourite ways of operating. Time terrorists hate change in working practices or, more importantly, they find it difficult to adapt to increases in workload and production speed. With computers and the Internet so readily available today, it has never been easier to obtain and transmit information. You can talk to people on the other side of the world, send drawings and text with great speed, yet the process can grind to a virtual halt when the person at the other end then has to disseminate the information, retrieve salient points and relay them to others. This will become the new skill for this century, and people will be paid well for this. As with the other type of terrorist, time terrorists will always be there, and we need to know how to deal with them.

As with all terrorists, the first thing is to be forewarned and ever vigilant. Identify them to all new members, and outline what they will try and do if given the chance. Always remember – they may seem nice and friendly,and they generally are – but like a dog, once a biter always a biter.

You can still work with them, and they will do some good work, but never take them into your confidence, and do not enter into talks or discussions with them concerning time management and work practices or you will be going around in circles for ever. If you can work without them, then do so. They generally never get too high up in a company due to the work-to-rule ethic they promote. When they do rise high in a company, it is generally as a sideline worker such as a union representative or a health and safety officer. This is not to say all of these people are time terrorists – as with all things, you should get to know people before making a judgement. And, again, do not be surprised if the nice person they all warned you about turns on you one day.

Practical tips for dealing with late people

- If you have a good time system in your diary and you have to meet with these people, always schedule them as your last item of the day, and give then no time overlap.
- Have other things to do when they do not turn up.
- Make them wait until you have completed the task in hand.
- Never be late for appointments with them.
- Give them a start and finish time for all meetings or involvements with them.
- Do not give them things to do that are time-critical.
- Give them a reminder of the appointment time well in

advance, and again near to the time.
- Do not make light of their rudeness; they will soon always be on time for you (but still late for everyone else).
- If you are able, teach them how to manage a diary.

Give them a copy of this book

SUMMARY

Time Terrorists will:

- Work against you whenever they can do so, directly or indirectly.
- Like to have off the record chats.
- Send a bewildering variety and a vast number of e-mails.
- Seem very friendly to your face.
- Always hanker for the way it used to be.
- Try to pick off the soft targets (new or young members of your team).
- Work hard at not working hard.
- Promise the earth and deliver mud.
- Be like the dog that has bitten once; never trust them with others.
- As the leopard, never change its spots.
- Like to use time, especially that of others.
- Not always be spotted at first.
- Prefer large organisations.
- Have much knowledge of other people's problems
- Think the company can always afford more money.

How to protect yourself and your team from them

- Patrol the perimeters; in other words, keep an eye on

your team.

- Do not involve them.
- Look out for new converters to the cause.
- Warn new and younger members of the team.
- Never confide in them.
- Get them to work for you not with you.
- Remember they like being the way they are.
- They will always be looking for soft targets.

The way we work with people is paramount to our own success now and in the future, so we must always be careful that we do not allow ourselves to become a terrorist.

If we are left off a project or do not get that promotion we wanted, it can be very easy to fall into the downward spiral of the terrorist and try to slow down projects and the efforts of others.

Everything happens for a reason and it is always positive even if at the time it may not seem like that way

Just pick yourself up, brush yourself down and move forward. This is a quality that will pay you great dividends in the future. For the many companies with whom I work, this is one of the rarest of attributes to find in others, and especially in younger managers.

EIGHT

TIME BANDITS

These people are the robbers and outlaws we probably think of when somebody mentions spaghetti westerns; the Mexicans with double bullet belts crossed over their chest. They will come down from the hills with whooperin', hollerin' and shooting into the air, only to be thwarted by a lone American in a poncho. You know the kind – slow but fast, never wanting to get involved, but always doing just that.

Or we may think of funny little men from the film *Time Bandits* by Terry Gilligan, charging around through time, up to no good and only out for their own gains. Whichever it may be, the result is the same, for chaos usually follows in their wake. It is precisely the same with our time bandits. They can be at any position in any company, though the higher up they are, the worse they can be for the individual. The main thing is to realise that with these people, it is not personal – they treat everyone the same... equally badly.

You know the type... picture this scenario: office, nice and quiet, everyone getting on with their work, and suddenly the time bandit arrives and bang! "Who took my file for Smith?" Everyone looks about, there might be a few shrugs and then they continue on with their work. "Okay, I will look for it myself then, shall I?" Everyone carries on working. Crash, bash, bang: "@#%*&*!! What are you lot doing? Help me look for it, they'll be here in five minuets." At this point everyone has to stop and help this incompetent to look for that which is not lost. The missing file, or whatever, generally turns up on their own, very untidy, desk.

The main thing with the time bandits is they are generally very busy people with no way of keeping time. They fight against being organised, as they like to give the appearance of being productive and the sense of being busy that disorganisation conveys to the observer. Of course, this is only in their own mind, as we, on the other side of the bandits' bad time habits, think they are inefficient, bumbling incompetents. In the main this is true, though it should be noted that in the context of team dynamics they can work well with others, and some of their other traits can be very useful.

But for now we are more concerned with the way they affect our own time management. If we are constantly stopping to help them find that which is not, in fact, lost, then a hole is created in our time planning. Or we are in some other way involved with the ensuing clean-up operation, much as you would after any natural disaster; rebuilding the lives of the office staff that are usually disrupted by the antics of the Time Bandit.

We have a choice with time bandits. We can:

1. Work with them.
2. Stay the hell out of town when we hear them coming.
3. Batten down the hatches and ride the storm, coming out only when the sun is shining again.

If the answer is that 'we work with them', then we need to know how to do this. It can be very simple if we know the basics and why they are the way they are. I have touched on the main reason for their simple lack of social skills; namely, that it is very easy for people to think that if we just get on and help them out, the quicker they will be gone. This is something these people rely on, day in and day out, every day of the year. With this knowledge in mind, we can organise them and give ourselves a peaceful life. Step one gets us close to the problem: *their lack of planning: do the planning for them* (take note if you are a Time Bandit and accept this help).

I am not suggesting we lie down for these people and let them walk all over us, as they seem to do in any event. No, what I am suggesting is that we can become very influential in planning the way in which these people use time. This does mean that we have to be very organised ourselves, so that we are able to help them get things done on time and to an acceptable standard that is expected of them (they do tend to set higher standards for others than they do for themselves). With this in mind, we are able to start to show them how to become better at time planning.

With diary management as the focus for our plan to help these people, we note that as they are very busy people, in the main, they do tend to have their diary to hand and to book in their appointments with plenty of notice. However, it all then falls down as they do not plan or properly schedule in the rest of their work around those appointments. Schedule a daily or weekly meeting with them. Talking through the work they have to do before the meeting is a good start, and then agree those things that you are able to do to help them. After agreeing these tasks, write them down and deliver your part. This may not seem as though it is your job, however, if it means that you are then in control of your workload and will not have them thrashing through the office door twenty minutes before the appointment, turning the place upside down looking for things and generally messing up your time management, then it has to be worth this effort.

Again, the practical things do not all have to be done by you. Once you know what is required, then you can delegate the tasks to others (delegation will be covered in a later chapter).

Practical Tips

1.   Plan your time.
2.   Help them plan their own.

3.   Agree to regular meetings (they generally keep meetings).
4.   Make sure that that 'it' is not lost by placing it in the right place at the right time.
5.   Take control of them.
6.   Keep them updated as to what is being done for them.
7.   Let them know that if they want your help, then their normal behaviour is not acceptable to you.
8.   Delegate tasks to others.
9.   Never overstep the line with them no matter how long the relationship, as they can always turn at any point. Respect is a big driving factor for the Time Bandit.

We now have them organised and on our side. This should allow us to become very time efficient and better able to attend to our own work.

"Stay the hell out of town when we hear them coming" may not be a very practical thing to do, as we may not always be out at the right time. It is also not always practical if we are office-based, and it can be extremely difficult for us to plan our own time if it is to be based on the erratic movements of someone else. Staying away also means that if you come in after it is all over, you will still lose time as the others will tell you what has just happened, though perhaps not be mentally able to assist very much as they are still likely to be traumatised. Another aspect of staying away is that when you do happen to be there on the odd occasion and you have got the timing wrong or they come in unexpectedly, you will get the full force of the treatment, as it will appear you are a 'new' face at which to have a go.

Battening down the hatches and riding the storm, coming out only when the sun shines again, also presents perils. In adopting this tactic, the Time Bandit will still disrupt your time while they are there thrashing about, and you can never manage to get right out of the way of these people. You generally will still have to wait for the dust to settle before you can fully continue with your work. The other side to all of these options is that they are not going to change, just get worse while we are looking to reduce stress caused by others. So the proactive approach is the key to our interaction with others.

SUMMARY

Time Bandits

- Delegate.
- Generally are very big producers or high flyers.
- Have a very well defined and high self-esteem.
- Their own belief system runs contrary to all others.
- Behave very much like Jekyll & Hyde.
- Involve others in their problems.
- Always look for that which is not lost.
- Very focused on one task being better than others (if only in their own mind).
- Are a must for any company to reach true potential as they are always challenging the norm.

How to protect your self and team from them

- Work with them.
- Never cross the line.
- Never try to avoid contact.
- Become part of their team.
- Get focused on the tasks with them.
- Spread their workload for them; diarise meetings to confirm action.
- Get yourself organised.
- Never let them step over the line with you.
- Understand them but do not come to tolerate them.

NINE

TIME ASSASSINS

This is a very strange category, as we can all be time assassins. We would normally think of an assassin as a professional paid killer, hired to do the dirty work – at a non-traceable distance – of others. They will stalk their target, get to know their movements and lie in wait for it to come into range, again, usually from a distance that suits a single bullet. The target is 'taken out' and off the assassin goes into anonymity. This is similar in some respects to the time assassins, who tend to be very close friends or work colleagues who may have been taking your time for years without you being aware.

One of the biggest problems with Time Assassins is that they are not always easily identifiable. Like most things in life, however, they do leave some trace as to where they have been, and you can then move them out of the prime time and into the down time. The main issue with Time Assassins is their ability to use your time without you realising it, and then not giving anything back. And, no, I don't believe all of our actions must be instantly rewarded, or even ever rewarded.

Remember, it is impossible to row someone over to the other side of the river without crossing yourself

The best thing is to look at the possible candidates for the job of our worst Time Assassins:

- Mum or Dad.
- Brothers and Sisters.

- Best Friends.
- Other people's best friends.
- Mobile Phones.
- Information Companies (timetables of any kind, the worst are usually trains).
- Internet.
- Work Colleagues.
- Telephone systems that put you on hold.
- Yourself.
- Your boss.
- Best enemies.
- Meetings.
- Late people.
- Your watch.
- Ill health.
- The alarm clock and a comfy bed.
- Procrastination.

The list can go on, but I think you get the drift. As with all the aspects of time that are discussed in this book, it may not be something that at first you wish to change. We all like to talk to our friends. But what if they like talk to you on the phone from work when they are on their lunch break and you are not – but they cannot take incoming calls when they are working. One hour a day, five days a week, 46 weeks of the year = 5.75 40 hour working weeks on the phone per year that may mean you are working at half capacity for that amount of time.

The Internet can be a very time destructive tool, and is used by most when they are at work and ostensibly doing other things. Most search engines come back with a million options that cover a billion subjects, although sometimes you are lucky and hit the right thing straight off.

Time Assassins are not always visible so they take up your time without you knowledge until it is too late. The work-related Time

Assassins are the people who due to their own lack of talent or desire to step up to the mark, ask you to come along and do team presentations or talks, or ask for your help on this and that as you have just the right skills to do the job. The phrase 'blowing smoke up your ass' is just about right for the Time Assassin, as they have this mastered and can make you feel like a million dollars at that moment. It may be years later when you realise that the time you gave freely was all on your time, and not needing any effort from their time. You run about the place like a headless chicken only to find out they are at home, or enjoying him- or herself on the golf range.

The non-work related Time Assassin could be even more destructive, as they are generally very emotionally linked to you. These people are very tiring, and at their very worst can break up marriages and bring extra strain to your already hectic life. The emotional effort they can exert can bring us down to our knees, and this is their equivalent of the real assassin's rifle that can pick us off from any distance. The problem is that, once again, at the time we do not think that they are undermining our own time and causing problems in our own relationships.

They are only asking you because so and so is very busy (I cannot ask John to take me to the shops, he is very busy; you know he is a doctor /lawyer) and you only work at the shop or office – as if your time is less than important and your life is more disreputable then the high-flying sibling. We all have our crosses to bear, but we don't have to be subjected to this type of time wasting. The only way you can get through this is to realise what is being done to you and to make the change so that you can be true to yourself and your time.

Every birth has one death; it is the time we spend in the middle where we need to come to grips with being aware that the Time Assassins can follow us from cradle to grave. It is how we get the time back that we give so freely and with good faith so that we have more control over our lives. The hardest thing to do is make the changes needed to get our lives back on track by understanding what it is we are looking to achieve. Planned goals are our biggest defence against the Time Assassins, as we no longer live our lives and do the things we want to do only because they let us. *Just because they gave you life does not give them the right to hound you to death.* The real work is to set out our goals and set the track so that when we are asked to bend over we can say no, but I can do it at another time, as it is better for me. It may be a real defining moment in our lives to realise that this is the only way to deal with the emotional Time Assassins; to give you the armour you need to live your life in a way that is best for you.

In this book I have a section on *smarter* action planning, and this is you best protection against the emotional Time Assassin. Having the plan and working the plan is about as good as it gets. In the past you may have buckled under the pressure of the emotional Time Assassin, but now we know where we are going and we understand who the Time Assassins are in our lives and how to deal with them.

SUMMARY

- The closest people to you are possibly the worst.
- Years can pass before you realise they are doing it to you.
- Assassins are only out to look after number one.
- Emotional blackmail is their preferred tool.

Protection from Time Assassins

- Never again let them take control.
- Understand that your time is more important to you than it is to them.
- Have a plan and work it.
- Make them fit into your time.
- Write down plans and goals and achieve them.
- Avoid them at work when ever possible.

TEN

TIME VANDALS

This is the penultimate of the time destructive groups of people that we are to meet. These people are the time chameleons. They cover all areas and are hard to overcome. The usual thought that comes to mind when we think of a vandal is a youth in a hood scuttling about in the dark, spraying words on anything in reach, smashing windows on broken buildings or smashing up bus stops. They have no real wish to join in with regular, organised society. To this end, we make our bus stops out of bombproof material rather then try and address the real issues. Because of this, the vandal does not see the suffering they cause in the trail of destruction that they leave in their wake.

Because they have the ability to blend into the background, it is very difficult to protect yourself. The thing is to be able to see their patterns, and learn how to overcome them. They have little regard for your time or their own. In their own mind they are not going to get anywhere in life, so why help others get something out of life? They are the black cloud, negative people in the extreme, and they never have a good word to say about anyone or anything.

It is always everyone else's fault; they are blameless in everything they do. If you show them how to do something once, you'll show them a hundred times until you find it easier to do the task yourself. This is their *modus operandi*.

Time Vandals are a very complex creature – as they have the ability to blend in we will always have to be on your guard when dealing with them, but deal with them we must even if it is to only warn them off. Their ability to look at all things negatively is very easy to overcome, as we just make them unhappy by being so positive about things that it makes them feel uncomfortable around us.

The very essence of good time management is that no matter what happens, we have the ability to overcome it positively. The Time Vandal is only effective short term – as long as we do not accept their behaviour when they are in our presence then we are protected from them. To this end, we have to recognise them from the pack.

SUMMARY

- Blend into the background, thus conspicuous by their own absences.
- Treat everyone with the same loathing and contempt, including themselves.
- Repeat offenders – they generally have no wish to take responsibility for their own actions, always expecting others to make up for them.
- Can be very manipulative before being discovered.
- Generally have little respect for anyone's time, so is usually late for most things, and then come ill-prepared as they did not have time.
- Are moved throughout a company, from work area to work area or department to department, just to get rid of them.
- Will be job hoppers.

Protection From Time Vandals

- Identifying the Time Vandal is the most important defence.

- Remove them from any time critical areas.
- Have your own robust Time Management system.
- Remain positive about your own outlook.
- Don't associate with them at or outside work, as their inability to separate life will always bring you into conflict over work issues when you want to be away from them.
- Don't try to change them – they are happy being unhappy!
- Spend time with Time Lords.

ELEVEN

TIME LORDS

These are the mystical people we have all heard about. At work we hear of Dave who works in such and such office as someone who will "go all the way." He is able to motivate his team and get them all working, but never seems to be in the office "I just don't know how he does it?"

Dave seems, on the surface, to have it all sewn up and, by and large, he will have. The difference with the likes of Dave is that they know what works and what does not. They take very little pressure from the top, as his seniors know he will deliver, so they leave him alone to get on with it. This is the first important lesson to learn from the Time Lord: be very, very good at what you do. To this end, you free up many hours that the rest of us have to spend in pointless meetings, answering questions on sales targets and other work-related issues.

Time Lords understand the true value of their own time, and that every minute must be maximised. They read all they can from those who are better than them, and they seek counsel from those who are at the top of their game, not from the self-opinionated no hopers who would make you believe they are the best. You know the sort that sit all day, achieving nothing and just wasting everyone else's time – the Time Terrorists. The Time Lord is where we are going to get you after you have finished reading this book. Until then, let us just examine what it is that makes them the way they are.

One thing is for certain; they were not born like it, and for most of them, they have been the worst timekeepers and work hamsters that have ever existed. Then someone turns on the light bulb and away they go; the change is dramatic. We can all improve at most things in life, and time management is one of the best places to start as it frees up the time needed to sort out all of the other areas. The Time Lord has the best of both worlds, because they are on top of their game – and because of that, people leave them alone. If they run teams they have more time to spend with their people, and because of this the people in the team feel needed and become more productive. They learn the time skills that the boss uses and emulate them, so they are able to complete more work with a higher degree of accuracy, as they are not under time pressure. This, in turn, means less stress, less time off sick, and less need to arrange cover, as you can see that this just spirals upwards with more and more time being freed up.

This is the secret of the Time Lord; the effort put in once is repaid over and over again. But as with all things, they still have to keep a tight control on time, and be very clever not to get drawn into other people's problems. There are others who are not prepared to put in the groundwork needed to become time self-sufficient, and who will always try and dump their unfinished work on the Time Lord.

If you can identify a true Time Lord, spend as much time as you possibly can to get to the bottom of their time problem-solving powers. You can have the makings of a true Time Lord. Just sit back for a moment and think of a life with no stress; a world that works at your own speed. A world where you never get tired and work just seems to be one great adventure, full of fun and enjoyment. There will be time to be at home with the family, with no nagging desire to get back and finish the work that was due ten days ago. This is the life of the Time Lord, and you can have it too... just read on.

SUMMARY

- They are very good at what they do.
- They have a very positive outlook that is infectious.
- They have a very time-efficient thinking process.
- They know that all time is important not just their own.
- They read and keep up-to-date with the lattest thinking in their chosen field.
- They are the same as everyone else – ordinary people doing extraordinary things
- Make it your life's work to spend as much time as possible building a mentor networking group of these people.

TWELVE

GETTING TO THE START

TIME RESPECT

Have you ever said, "If I had more time or money I would be able to..." or "Some day I will do this..." As we know, someday island is just a fantasy island where things never happen and dreams lay shattered on the shore. Then one day you will look around and say, "Where did the time go? What happened to my life?" This is why it is so important to embrace the ideas in this book, and work to improve your own understanding of time management – time shifting – as something that can, and will, change your life forever.

Let's get down to some practical ways in which you can improve your time keeping, letting everyone with whom you come in contact know that now you are in control of time and have lots of it – to do the things *you* want to do.

Let's start off with the watch. As I said earlier, it is the most time destructive implement ever invented. If we write a list of the places where we can check the time, you will find it is quite lengthy:

1.   Other people.
2.   The radio.
3.   The car.
4.   The mobile phone.
5.   The TV.
6.   The computer.

7.   The clock on the wall.
8.   The fax machine.
9.   The car radio.
10.   The heating system timer.
11.   The TV timetable.
12.   Most electrical equipment.
13.   Microwave.
14.   Cooker.
15.   Hi-fi systems.

This list is only here to prompt you; I am sure you add to it. We can even get a close feel for the time out of the window just by the amount of light outside. The trouble with the watch is we get conditioned from an early age to keep looking at it. The first time we get a watch we look at it, yet we go around asking people the time just so they will say "I thought you were wearing a watch?" "Oh! Yes I have, and it is x o'clock!"

With a great smile on our faces we then become conditioned to looking at it. Have you ever had this conversation with someone with whom you are in a meeting: "Boring you am I?" "No! Why do you ask?" "It's just that you have looked at your watch six times in the past few minutes." "Sorry, force of habit!" Force of habit or not, it is still the same; it's very rude, because what you are saying to someone is that you are not sufficiently interested in them to show them time respect. *Time respect is the most important lesson you can learn in life – it will give you a better relationship with everyone you come in to contact with... and more importantly, with our loved ones.*

This is also very negative. If you are involved in sales, you may have a number of meetings that day and you are literally busting a gasket to get to this appointment, but now you are worried about making the next appointment, so all of this meeting is spent looking at your watch and worrying about the next one. This does two things to the prospective clients you are meeting: (1) it makes them not trust you as you look shifty; and (2) you are giving them the idea that they are not as important to you as the next person you have lined up for a meeting. All of this comes just from looking at your watch. It will also make them think that you are not going to be able to meet your commitments if they give you the order.

And if they need to get hold of you, are you going to be there, or able to return their calls? This will be the same even if it is not a sales call; even meetings with friends – this type of behaviour will make them feel that you are not that interested in them. If you want people to like you, listen to them. In the U.S. the biggest growth industry over the past decades has been in shrinks, counsellors and psychologists, who just sit there and listen to people talking about their problems – they say a problem shared is a problem halved. The art to life is share your time with people without taking up their time. This may seem like a play on words, but if we can be in the moment then we are going to get more out of it. People like to talk about themselves. We are no different, or are we? I believe that we need to be adaptive. We are here to find out as much about others with the least possible effort, so learning to ask the right questions can make you seem very interested, but also helps you get to the information that you need.

You can move on or stay until we are happy with the answers we have so that our meeting has achieved everything we wanted and did not take any longer than needed.

Respect for time is the single most important thought of our day. Am I receiving it? Am I giving it? The whole point to this statement is that if we have no respect for others or ourselves, then we can become Time Vandals. This may seem like a strong statement, but think about it. A Time Vandal has no respect for their own time, so why would they have any respect for that of others? Vandals in the normal sense have no respect for the property of other people, and have no sense of the bigger community, so they will scrawl graffiti on things or break things, never really taking in the big picture in terms of the consequences of their actions. Society is then left to pick up the consequences. All as a result of a mindless act from someone with no real sense of their own importance, thinking the world owes them, as they don't have all the things they see on TV, and thinking the Government or some faceless corporation is withholding it from them. Yet if they were to see the big picture they would realise the vast sums of money spent on policing and clearing up after their vandalism could be spent on the greater community in which they live, to bring about a better standard of living. Now you may be thinking, what has this got to do with not wearing a watch?

It is only meant to illustrate that the watch can have the same effect, by distracting you from the real issues. We must get used to *time* verses *task* efficiency. If we have a list of tasks needed to complete in a day, then we have a starting point.

The best to-do list you will ever have is one that you can't read at the end of the day, as all things will have been crossed off and completed.

THIRTEEN

DIARY PLANNING

How to use an agenda time planning diary, one of the best on the market, is the Positive Forward life planning system, as it incorporates a number of simple systems in one.

The first thing to do is a review of our own time and how it is planned. If we take some time and review our diaries, if we have one then that's a step in the right direction. I will assume for now that you have some sort of diary system, and you use it on a regular basis. With the activities review sheet on page 62, follow the headings and write in the time spent on each. Add in your own if there are specific things that are peculiar to your own work or home life, but do not make it to elaborate. All we are after in the main is to identify the actual planned tasks that are in our diaries prior to them happening.

Write the time spent in blue if it was in the diary before and in red if it was added as a reminder after the event. If it is not written in the diary but you know you did it, then it just goes into the 'Stuff' column.

By completing this task, we discover that as with most people, the diary is used for recording events after they have happened, or they fall into the 'Stuff' column as they have not been properly diarised.

Now we have an idea of our current situation regarding time management, we are able to move forward and start to plan the rest of our lives in a competent time management system.

Personal Review of Organised Time

Name_____

Date Review carried Out_____

Week	Time on Phone	Group Meetings	Courses	Meetings Held By you	Time on Computer	Travel	Stuff	Specific Work only you can d	Reviewing Time Management	Others	Hours Worked this week
1											
2											
3											
4											
5											
6											
7											
8											
9											
10											
Totals											
Hours											
% time											

Thus by having a review every 10 weeks we are able to maintain a high level of stability in our time management systems.

The process of using a diary is very complex, and can be the best way of running a time efficient system. Most people will have a diary of sorts – most will have a just a simple book that has the days in it marked out with useful information about the moon and bank holidays. Yet it invariably has no real time planning use, as few have timed sections in them.

If we are to progress forward then we need to have a system that lets us allocate not only the day a task is to be completed on, but also a time slot that can incorporate a start and a finish time. A truly advanced diary system will run on a rolling 3-year basis, so that we have the ability to plan for major events well in advance. This gives the time planner the ability to work back from the point in the future. Back to a point now so that we have the ability to break down even the most complicated of tasks into small points and plan them in. Much like an Olympic athlete will have the event day and time in their diary four years in advance, with a work schedule depicting the events that will happen on which days over the period so as to be in peak condition for the day of the event. Each step is as important as the next, as without meticulous planning they will never perform at a truly amazing level.

Our lives are not a trial – we are here for real, so we need to plan if we truly wish to be exceptional in life by our words and actions.

We must start off with a long-term goal, then work it back. As you can see from the *Day-Book*, we have goals set out that we have set time limits on. This way we can then work back from when we want to have achieved it by to the actions we need to have completed each day. With a time management system in place we now need some instruction on how best to use it. We need to start with our own personal time set in stone, around which every thing else ideally will fit.

Starting with our personal time is very important so that we know how much of the day we have left in which to work. Now for many people they do not have the ability as they see it to do this, as they have set times in which they have to be in the office. We do have control over the rest of the time that is not taken up with work. Start with weekends and evenings if you need to just to get an idea of how to use the time that is ours. The truly enlightened Time Lord will have his weekends planned as well as his weekdays.

If you have a family that needs to have lifts to this and that, I would suggest that you have a house diary that everyone is encouraged to write in, including you, so that everyone has the ability to time plan around events. This will also get your children used to time management, which will put them ahead of many of their peers once out into the work place, and may even help them with planning exam revision.

Back to our main diary. Each day we have the top section that, as indicated, has the main key tasks for the day usually off the daily task sheet. These can then be crossed off as we complete them. If you have the full system then only use the one planning sheet – if you just carry a diary then put them in both so that you can remain focused on the main daily tasks. The diary sets out in 15 minute sections the day from 06.30–22.00 hrs. This should cover most of the day you'll be active and need to plan. You'll find that as you work on time management your ability to schedule events will improve, to the extent that you have the ability to allocate the exact amount of time needed to complete each task. The heart of the system is that you have goals to work on – time is then allocated to accomplish all the tasks.

You now have the basics of your new time management system –

by working on this every day you can start to see the stress go as you have the confidence to say no to the people that you can identify as not being helpful in your new time-efficient life, and you'll have the time to achieve all of the things you once wished for.

If you work in an office environment, then the more people that you get involved in using this system, the better your own time management can become.

Area of Focus _____ ST ☐ LT ☐

Narrative Explanation

Date to be Achieved _____

Date Achieved _____

Signature _____

Review Comments

Date _____

Picture / Photo

Benefit /Advantage/ Reward/ Merit of achieving objective

Affirmation_____

Monday 1 Main Tasks	Tuesday 2 Main Tasks	Wednesday 3 Main Tasks	Thursday 4 Main Task	Friday 5 Main Task	Saturday 6 Main Task	Sunday 7 Main Task	Notes:
------------------	------------------	------------------	------------------	------------------	------------------	------------------	------------------
------------------	------------------	------------------	------------------	------------------	------------------	------------------	------------------
------------------	------------------	------------------	------------------	------------------	------------------	------------------	------------------
------------------	------------------	------------------	------------------	------------------	------------------	------------------	------------------
06.30	06.30	06.30	06.30	06.30	06.30	06.30	------------------
07.00-----------	07.00-----------	07.00-------------	07.00----------	07.00-----------	07.00-----------	07.00----------	------------------
30	30	30	30	30	30	30	------------------
08.00----------	08.00----------	08.00-------------	08.00----------	08.00-----------	08.00----------	08.00----------	------------------
30	30	30	30	30	30	30	------------------
09.00-----------	09.00-----------	09.00-------------	09.00----------	09.00-----------	09.00-----------	09.00----------	------------
30	30	30	30	30	30	30	
10.00-----------	10.00-----------	10.00-------------	10.00----------	10.00-----------	10.00-----------	10.00----------	
30	30	30	30	30	30	30	
11.00-----------	11.00-----------	11.00-------------	11.00----------	11.00-----------	11.00-----------	11.00----------	
30	30	30	30	30	30	30	Contacts:
12.00-----------	12.00-----------	12.00-------------	12.00----------	12.00-----------	12.00-----------	12.00----------	------------------
30	30	30	30	30	30	30	------------------
13.00-----------	13.00-----------	13.00-------------	13.00----------	13.00-----------	13.00---------	13.00---------	------------------
30	30	30	30	30	30	30	------------------
14.00-----------	14.00-----------	14.00-------------	14.00----------	14.00-----------	14.00---------	14.00----------	------------------
30	30	30	30	30	30	30	------------------
15.00-----------	15.00-----------	15.00-------------	15.00----------	15.00-----------	15.00---------	15.00----------	------------------
30	30	30	30	30	30	30	------------------
16.00-----------	16.00-----------	16.00-------------	16.00----------	16.00-----------	16.00---------	16.00----------	------------------
30	30	30	30	30	30	30	------------------
17.00-----------	17.00---------	17.00-------------	17.00----------	17.00-----------	17.00---------	17.00----------	----
30	30	30	30	30	30	30	
18.00-----------	18.00-----------	18.00-------------	18.00----------	18.00-----------	18.00---------	18.00----------	Main weekly Tasks:
30	30	30	30	30	30	30	------------------
19.00-----------	19.00-----------	19.00-------------	19.00----------	19.00-----------	19.00---------	19.00----------	------------------
30	30	30	30	30	30	30	------------------
20.00-----------	20.00-----------	20.00-------------	20.00----------	20.00-----------	20.00-----------	20.00----------	------------------
30	30	30	30	30	30	30	------------------
21.00-----------	21.00----------	21.00-------------	21.00----------	21.00-----------	21.00-----------	21.00-----------	------------------
30	30	30	30	30	30	30	------------------
22.00-----------	22.00-----------	22.00-------------	22.00-----------	22.00-----------	22.00---------	22.00-----------	------------------
Task list events for following day.	Task list events for following day.	Task list events for following day.	Task list events for following day.	Task list events for following day.	Task list events for following day.	Task list events for following day.	------------------
------------------	------------------	------------------	------------------	------------------	------------------	------------------	------------------
------------------	------------------	------------------	------------------	------------------	------------------	------------------	-------

FOURTEEN

TASK LISTS

One part of an effective time management system is the task list. The system (see page 70) will help you to organise your day, and should be ideally completed in the main at the end of the day as your last task, and should only take about ten minutes to complete, yet may save hours of lost time the next day.

It is a very simple system, and when used with other time management systems, will save you a great deal of stress and, of course, time.

TOP LEFT – MAIN TASKS OF THE DAY

By defining what is to be achieved tomorrow we are starting to bring the future in to our own realities today. It also starts us to think about how much time we should allocate to each task. I would suggest that you add a time of the day that we are more likely to be able to archive the task in the most time efficient way possible. If it involves a phone call, is that person available to talk at a particular time of the day. I always clarify a time of the day when I will best be able to contact someone, and make it as if it were an appointment in the diary. I will also, whenever possible, do the same with others that need to call me I will always suggest a time to take calls and then set aside the small tasks for that time. Time allocation is very important If you have large task that you know will take all of the day then don't set other tasks on the list – it is better to have one task and complete it than to have a number on the go never fully completed.

Daily Task List

Main Tasks of the Day

1. _____
2. _____
3. _____
4. _____
5. _____
6. _____
7. _____
8. _____
9. _____
10. _____

Contact List for the day

1. _____
2. _____
3. _____
4. _____
5. _____
6. _____
7. _____
8. _____
9. _____
10. _____

Carry over Tasks

1. _____
2. _____
3. _____
4. _____
5. _____
6. _____
7. _____
8. _____

Small Tasks

1. _____
2. _____
3. _____
4. _____
5. _____
6. _____
7. _____
8. _____
9. _____
10. _____
11. _____
12. _____
13. _____
14. _____

New Tasks

1. _____
2. _____
3. _____
4. _____
5. _____
6. _____
7. _____
8. _____
9. _____
10. _____
11. _____
12. _____
13. _____
14. _____
15. _____

TOP RIGHT – CONTACT LIST OF THE DAY

By having the numbers we need to use on the one piece of paper, it saves us time when we are moving from one task to another. As the day progresses, the numbers that we need are there so we have no need to rummage through lots of files for numbers – we also do not have to stop and access other databases, all of which take time.

This list may again need to be updated as we move through the day – as we are more used to using this system you will be surprised how effective you can become.

BOTTOM LEFT – SMALL TASKS

By having an easily accessible list of small things that we need to complete, we have a very effective system for filling in tasks that we always put off, as they are small and do not have a key critical event surrounding them. For most of us, we may store them up and dedicate a whole day to doing these things. That is okay, but words of warning – as we are doing things that we have no real wish to do, we generally end up not using the whole day as planned. We can waste a day and still not complete all of the small tasks that we set out to do. Yet by having a list of small tasks, it may help in a few ways:

1. Each task completed gives us a burst of physical and mental energy.
2. Gives us a flexible workload so that we have small tasks to complete – if we are stuck waiting for an answer to a larger task then we then have other things to be going on with.
3. Keep a number of small tasks to complete after lunch, or when we are at our lowest part of the daily physical/ mental cycle.

Small tasks need to be planned, as they are very stressful when we put them off – they just sit there nagging away, usually once we are home and trying to relax.

BOTTOM RIGHT NEW TASKS

Invariably, with each task that we accomplish a new one will replace it. This can again take you by surprise, so by adding these new tasks as they arrive, we can see if we can piggy-back them onto our current list of ongoing tasks. It also gives us a reminder for later that we have other things that we are contracted to do. If you then review these at the end of the day, you are able to check that you are not just taking on other people's monkeys. I suggest that you also keep your lists and review then periodically to see if we are not just duplicating lives in a never-ending ring of unproductive tasks.

CENTRAL CARRY OVER TASKS

It is very important to realise that we are never likely to complete every task that we set ourselves on the day on which we decided to do them. So we need to have a place to put our new set of tasks that we can add to our next day's list. These can come from any of the four other sections, or just straight in from a new task that we will have to park straight away.

Carry over tasks are a key area that we can use to keep us focused on our overall goals.

FIFTEEN

QUESTIONS, QUESTIONS
HOW WE CAN IMPROVE OUR
TIME EFFICIENCY BY ASKING
THE RIGHT QUESTIONS

As we can see from the diagram below, there is a very easy way to set questions if you know what each of these statements mean and the words that can be added to it to arrive at the results we are after. The less time you take to get to the answer yet have people believe you are genual interested in them will take less time. Working from top to the right then to the bottom then back up to the left.

SUMMARY

1.   Initial question or opening statement:

   • "Tell me how you feel about this?"

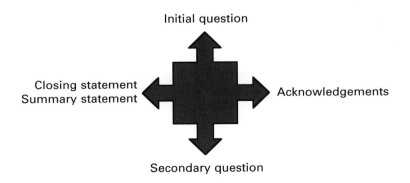

- "How do you think this will go?"
- "When do you think you will have the answer?"
- "What do you want the out come to be from our meeting?"
- "Can you see any other way of achieving this?"
- "Where do you see the help coming from?"
- "Why do you think that is going to work?"

2. You can also have a small opener but this can get cumbersome:

- "I would like to ask you how???????"
- "Your views are important to me tell me how???????"
- "So (Name), how do you feel this is going?????"

3. Never use these as a cop out:

- "Can I ask you...?"
- "Could you please?"
- "Would you please?"
- "Is it alright if I enquire?"

These just make you seem a bit slow in the minds of others, but believe me they will not even know that is the reason they are not connecting with you.

ACKNOWLEDGEMENT

That we acknowledge someone when having a conversation lets the other person know you are interested in what they say, so they are more free with their words. In this way, we are able to get to the point of our conversion with ease and pinpoint accuracy, and thus less time is spent. This can be as simple as a nod of the head or just agreeing by saying things

- "Oh yes I see"
- "I agree"
- "Ok"
- "Yes"

Usually, and naturally, we do this combined with a movement of the head or hands.

SECONDARY QUESTION

This is a vital part of the question cycle – it allows the other person to confirm that you were listening. It is also gets us to the real information:

- "That's an interesting question, tell me why did you ask me that?"
- "I have never been asked that before, why did you ask me that?"
- "Can you just elaborate on that for me; I just want to clarify my own thinking?"
- "That's interesting – can you just give me some more information on that?"

As you can see, it brings the other person in so that we can be under no misunderstanding as to what is being talked about. It will also make them really want to talk to you because you listen to them.

CLOSING STATEMENT/SUMMARY STATEMENT

This is the end of the cycle, and it gives you chance to convey your understanding of the questions and answers. This cycle is so vitally important when delegations of tasks are required for both sides, but mainly from your side if you are the one who is doing the delegating:

- "Just so I can make sure I have it right..."
- "What you are saying is..."
- "If I can deliver it in white will you give me the order..."
- "You need this by then..."
- "As I thought, what you mean is..."
- "I was sure that was what you were after..."
- "Given what you have just said, will Wednesday be all right?"

As you can see, whether it is a delegated task or an order from a prospective buyer, you can confirm that you have both fully understood what is needed, and so there is no need to spend time later going over what answers were given during a far off and long forgotten conversation.

All problems with the delegation of tasks can generally be traced back to a misunderstanding in the original conversation, and will become great sources of stress in the future.

BARTERING

When we interact with others we are able to seek help with our tasks and possibly help others with theirs. This a core fundamental time management technique, *bartering* what you have that I want with that you may wish to have that I have. Time tasks can be bartered in this way if you are good at something that takes you no time, yet takes someone else twice as much time.

By using the right questions, the other person may feel that they are being helpful, and not made to feel that you are putting on them or that they are inadequate. Time spent with others in your life gaining a greater understanding of what they are good at.

They say "If you love what you do for a living then you will never work a day in your life". So identify others that can be helpful and then find out how you can be helpful to them. WIN–WIN.

DELEGATION

This is one of the most fundamental tasks that we may do on a regular basis, whether it be parent to child or MD to other board directors. The desired outcome is always the same: *blind obedience* of the task delegated. In other words, you expect the task to be carried out how you envisaged it to be in your mind. This is where a great deal of conflict starts even before the task is carried out. We can see from our question cycle that we can now conduct a conversation in a manner that allows us to get to the right end result.

Delegation must start in much the same way:

1.   Know what we require as the completed task, e.g. have a vision for the peace of work and how you would like it carried out.
2.   Know the limitations of the person you are asking to carry out the work, and if they require help (so have diaries regular review meetings for large tasks, or even a head around the door from time to time to see if they are on top of the task – be mindful of point 6 below).
3.   Communicate the desired outcome as well as the task and the timescales.
4.   Set timescales that allow the task to be completed and which give you some leeway if the task is not completed on time.

5. Ask for conformation that the request has been fully understood and accepted, and timescales agreed.

6. Let them get on with the task, and only check on progress if agreed and near to the deadline.

7. With long-term complex cases, contract with the other person(s) both having a copy. (See the four section contract opposite.)

8. Give prase for a job well done, and only open and constructive feedback if not to the standard you had both agreed. (Point 5 or review contract point 7.)

As we can see from the four section contract on page 81, we can get a very complex task down to the main points, have a file that is both ready to hand that is agreed and signed. You will be amazed at how once belligerent people just get on with a task once it has been agreed in this way. Remember as a word of caution that this is not a tool to beat up others for not competing tasks by deadlines. Even if they work for you and you are paying someone specifically to do a certain kind of work (e.g. secretarial), they are fundamentally:

Doing your work for you

Thus we need to make sure we communicate effectively from day one about our standards and the expectations we have. Delegated tasks relieve a great deal of time, and the stress these tasks carry, yet if we don't carry out each of the steps while delegating tasks, we are just transferring the time and stress from now to a point in the future. The problem is that anything not paid for at the point of purchase incurs interest, so we not only get back the task incomplete, or not competed to an acceptable standard, we get back the stress but as our timescales are now shorter we get the stress back plus interest. The art of delegation is a very fine one to master, and Time Lords are masters of delegation.

My job:

In this box you write the agreed review actions that you are going to take forward from the meeting. These will include diarised review dates; it will also include any actions you have to do e.g. supply them with the figures or other information needed to complete the task.

You may also agree to make the appropriate contacts to help the person to gather facts for themselves to help them with your work.

Remember it is you work being carried out on your request and behalf by others.

Review details:

In this box we add our ongoing review comments and agree any changes in that are to de made to the original contract. This box is very important as:

What gets monitored gets done.

So be very careful to express any problems both sides may be having with the work while there is a chance to save time from being wasted when too much has been completed. The only thing that is discussed at these meetings it the task and the task only. It can be carried out as part of other one-to-one meetings just make sure there is no cross over or conflicts of interest.

Your Job
This is were they agree to the task being delegated and what they are going to do to complete the task effectively.

This can include format as well as amount of work that is excepted, time scales and other relevant information.

Date: _____

Signatures:

_____

_____

Any review changes should also be resigned.

_____

_____

Date: _____

_____

_____

Date: _____

SIXTEEN

THE DAYBOOK TASK LIST

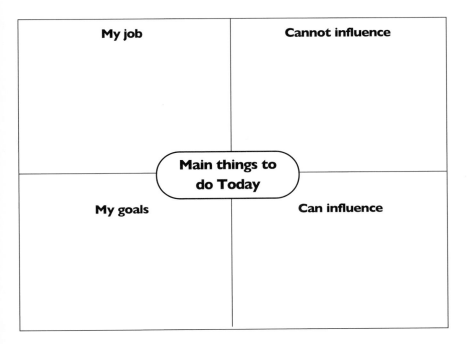

This table will give you the working tools to use when you set your time to one side. We will use an example of your work, but you can use the task list for any purpose.

MY job

This is your task list for things that need to be achieved to attain your goals. But, first it is always good to reaffirm your job task. Why are you being employed, and what is expected of you? If you cannot answer this then you need to take the time to review your job description, or take time with your line manager or supervisor. Without this information you will never be an effective employee or employer.

MY goals

This is what you go to work for; what you are tying to achieve. It may be completely different from the list in my job, but if you do not have a goal list that you are working to, then this will always lead to inefficient use of time and to many of the stress-related conditions that are prevalent in the workplace today. You only need to have a few at the start. It may be that you are looking for a place on the main board of directors, which will take you five years – then you can break down the work that can be done towards this over that time. These goals can be achieved – you will be shown how in Chapter 17 on goal setting.

Cannot Influence

Once again, this is the most impossible area that we get involved in every day, and it can be very time destructive, costing the commercial world billions every year. We tell everyone how badly they have got it wrong, and if only they had done it like this, things would be so much better. Remember, if your goal is to be a main board director, then one day they may be saying this about you. If we write these things down, we can see clearly whether we can move [can influence] them into what we want. In moving them, not just the act of writing it down, you can release yourself from their never ending time wasting potential.

Can influence

These are the platforms from which you can take action. They stem from the other sections, or they may be original and new, but they give you great power over your time tasks and, in themselves, can give you things to do that may even be added to your short-term goal list. It is very important that we spend time contemplating this area, as it will be the linchpin of your daily task list.

Main things to do today

This area will be your short 'get on to and do today' list. By spending ten to fifteen minutes each day as part of your quiet time in getting this list down to five items a day, this will be more powerful than you can imagine for taking control of your time. We can then get you working more effectively than you are at present.

These items can be added to your to-do list for the day (I will cover to-do lists later in this chapter). The main purpose of this task is to focus on those issues for which you can make a difference today. These may change from day to day, or they may remain the same, but just by writing them down you are ahead of the game by about 98% of the population. This may sound like it's all we need to do, but if it were we would all have been football stars or astronauts, or had a pony when we were children. It is much more than this; you have to bring the goals into the real world so that you can act on them.

The key to this task it is to move from external to internal motivators, as we know that external motivators only give you a movement similar to a ball when kicked. It only moves for a short time, then needs to be kicked again to keep the momentum, but it is also erratic, with a quick pace to start and then slowing down. Even if it is being dribbled it is still speeding up and then slowing down. In time management it is extremely inefficient and tiring to just keep waiting to be kicked and kicked again, just to get from A to B – and if the kicker has a bad day or is not there, then everything stops. If we can internalise the motivation, then we can keep an even pace and maintain it forever.

This is one of the key skills we need to acquire if we are to become time masters. To this end, we can go through some of the outcomes from our quiet time and our goal plans. They will give us these internal motivators, and thus help us to keep time in our heads and fit time to the task, not the task to the time. So, by having a shortlist of the things to do from our daybook task list, we then can work on our own priorities at the same time as achieving the priorities we may need to accommodate of others. This is a reflection of the true sense of the purpose of this book, which is to bring things back on to an even keel, centred and focused on the detail while at the same time maintaining an overview of the big picture.

The following task list is much more than your conventional to-do listing or 'look at me, I am busy' list. If used properly, a to-do list is really effective; if not it is like most things we do – convenient but not overly productive. So let's look at how we can use this task list. Bear in mind that its application and benefits apply equally to whatever issue or objective is relevant to your situation. This task book system does allow you to time plan more effectively, as you know with pinpoint accuracy what you are working towards with the time you're releasing from other areas, and gives a sense of purpose.

The table on page 85 is an example many people like to start with – the time savings they have made.

As you can see anything can go on one of these daybook task lists. It takes no time to do, but will achieve so many positive things in your life that you will be truly amazed.

My job	**Cannot influence**
Lose weight	Genetic makeup
Get from size 18 to 12	Years of bad diet
Reduce from 16 stone to 10.5 stone	How I was brought up
Achieve this in 12 months	Other peoples' view of me
Join a gym	Lack of help from others so far
Join diet club	Advertising enticing me to eat the
	wrong things
Healthy eating	Bad food that tastes so good
Use the mirror (not scales) every day	

Main Things to do Today
1. Be happy with being me as I am today and in 12 months – maintain positive outlook
2. Select main foods and snacks for the day
3. 20 minutes at the gym
4. Closure of all self-limiting beliefs

My goals	**Can influence**
Lose weight	What I eat
Get from 16 to 10.5 stone	Time in the gym
Reduce from size 18 to 12	Maintain positive outlook
To be achieved in 12 months from	My own internal belief system and
today	outlook on life
Live a happy life as a slim person	Stop raking over past
	Other people to help me
	What my children and family eat
	My external appearance (clothes only,
	not cosmetic surgery)

SEVENTEEN

S.M.A.R.T.E.R. GOAL SETTING

S.M.A.R.T. is an acronym that many people will be aware of, but may not be sure what it means. What do you think it means?

- S   = Specific
- M   = Measurable
- A   = Achievable
- R   = Realistic
- T   = Timed

How about this one?

S.M.A.R.T.E.R. Will be where most people get to: "where does the E.R come in" they say? Well, if you are working on timed items the SMART acronym is of no use, so let me explain:

- S   = Stretching
- M   = Motivational
- A   = Actionable
- R   = Review able
- T   = Time bound
- E   = Evidenced
- R   = Reviewed

To start, the difference between the two versions is that one is restrictive in its own right, and can be done for you, with little input from you, whereas my version can only be achieved with your input, and is best done by you, for you. You can have more than one running at a time, and the input for each will usually come from your daybook task list. These goal orientated action plans will take you through the day and get you where you want to go. Without an action plan to review, then time management can slip and you will inevitably be off key and out of kilter with life. We have to make sure that if we want to achieve a life of mastery over time, then our words and actions agree.

In separating the components of the acronym, I will explain how they are used to achieve a workable task reminder.

S = Stretching

To achieve great things the long-term goal is exemplified by stretching, and then we break it down into bite size pieces. *How do you eat an elephant? Bite by bite.* That is the problem with many of these plans; they do not give you a big enough challenge. They are not really what you want so you lose motivation. This is why most of these action plans are forced on us, and never achieve the outcomes promised. Yes, they do need to be specific, but that is achieved by the other parts of the acronym. They say that a rut is just a grave with the ends kicked out. If we do not set ourselves targets that inspire us and make us question whether we can do it or not, then those targets are neither stretching nor challenging. If it does not inspire us, then we will never last the course when the going gets tough and we are looking for the easy way out. With most of these things, people say that a realistic goal should be set so that it can be achieved. But we are not looking to be like everyone else, we are looking to master the challenges of time.

M = Motivational

You are the only one who can decide if it is motivational but, again, we need to think about what is behind the motivator. If you ask most people if they get paid enough they will say no. We would all like more money – or would we? If you think about it, we do not just want more money; it is the things we can spend it on that we really want, so we need to be very careful in challenging our motivations. Share them with someone else – your partner or mentor – but we must only share them with people who will help us, not try to help us to fail... and believe me, there are more people who will be trying to do that than those trying to help you achieve your goals. When we review this part of the plan every day, we should still feel good and our motivators should fill us with passion and pride, even a year or more later, and especially on achieving each small part.

A = Actionable

If the words we use when we set our action plan are not descriptive or meaningful to us, we cannot take action on them. It is imperative that we fully understand that unless we get this part of our planning right, we are not going to get the results we want. If time is to be mastered we need to be able to move forward on the issues we are currently having trouble with. If the plan has both action and motivation in the key areas, we get what could be termed *motiveaction*. This is easy to internalise, and gets truly outstanding results. Time can be tamed now that we have the tools to get more done.

R = Review able

If we cannot review a plan then it is not going to get us where we want to go. Remember, *what gets monitored gets done*. This part of the plan needs to be set out, and will impact greatly on the next part, time bound. This is where we set out to check that the plan makes sense. Can we look at the parts of the plan and judge that we are on plan, ahead of plan or behind plan? This is the most innovative part of the plan, and what sets it apart from the normal action plan or SMART plan that most of us will have had thrust upon us at some time or another.

T = Time bound

If we do not have a time scale, then the whole thing can fall into a rut. This component should involve the review of gaps and the end date.

This does not mean that if it is not completed by the end time specified we stop. All we need to do is set a new end date. Remember we are only after outcomes; results, good or bad, it makes no difference most of the time. They say that Edison tried to make the electric light bulb 2000 times before he got it right. When asked how he kept going after his failures, he replied that every time he did not get the desired outcome, he knew one more way of not making the light bulb, so his desired outcome was one step closer.

This is really such an important key. Did you fail you driving test the first time you tried? Yes, probably. But do you drive safely today because you were able to review your plan and the desired outcome, adjust the missing or incorrect actions and try again? We can only fail at anything once we give up; up until that point we are still in the game, as they say. However, do not interpret this as permission to become eternal procrastinators because we think "Oh well, I don't have to try or put in a special effort as I can always do it again". The time scale needs to be both realistic and motivational. If the plan is to, say, lose five stones in weight, then we cannot achieve this in three months. It may need to be possibly over a two or three year period. However, we can set monthly, weekly and daily review dates to plot our progress. The golden rule with weight loss is that it is not going to come off much faster than it went on if it is to stay off!

E = Evidenced

If we are unable to evidence what we are trying to activate, then it cannot be seen in the reality, so reality cannot change quickly enough. To this end we need to have things written down in a way that suits the task we are completing. We will cover all of the types of formats in the rest of this chapter, but for now, let's just concentrate on 'evidenced', by which we mean what evidence can you produce to back up the claim that you are going to, or are already doing, the things that your are committed to in the SMARTER Action Plan. Taking better time management, for example, are you using a proper diary management system such as the one described in this book? Or do you use a different type? This is not the real question but rather, we are asking, do you have a diary? I am not the biggest fan of these new palm top diaries, even though they do allow others to pro-gramme your diary for you and, as you will read later, this is a TIME LORD'S best weapon in our fight to gain time. But for now let's concentrate on the task at hand. If you do not have a diary then can you evidence somewhere that you have a shopping trip booked or you have an order slip to show that a matter has been dealt with? You will soon get used to doing this sort of thing. If you do have a diary, can you evidence that it is being used to the fullest advantage and that all the things you require are diarised in it? The stronger the evidence, the greater the chance of achieving the goals set out in the plan.

R = Reviewed

Reviewing the plan is the last part – or is it? We need to understand that throughout the process of setting up the plan we are reviewing it, and questioning it, and asking ourselves as to whether it will take us to our desired outcome or not. Can we relate to the plan and visu-alise ourselves completing it? We then need to review it regularly, depending on the type of plan and its detail. For most plans we will have broken it down into bit-sized chunks and, to this end, we should-if possible-have it separated it down further into small daily tasks. With time management this is certainly a requirement. We need to keep reminding our subconscious mind on the task that we are asking it to perform with the constant drip, drip of reinforcing evidence as to how well or otherwise we are doing. It is only with this management; the reinforcement and evaluation of our efforts that we can ever hope to achieve the desired outcomes.

We can use the analogy of the ship's captain who sets sail from England to go to New York. He knows that if he steers straight he will end up in Mexico or somewhere south of the intended target. As the ship cruises the high seas, the wind, waves and tides are all pushing the ship off course, so the pilot at the helm is constantly making small corrections to the ship's course so that an all safe and sound landing is achieved at the desired destination, without any problems. The principle that underpins any action plan is identical to the action taken by the ship's captain. However SMART the action plan that is thrust upon us, it usually gets put into the drawer and never sees the light of day again until the person who set it up comes to check on its progress. We whip it out and make all of the excuses as to why it never worked and why it was never going to work; the outcome being that we are let off the hook and we set up another new and updated plan.

Remember this next time you are arguing the toss over some meaningless point that you have not completed within the stipulated time frame. I have worked with people who will spend more time and effort making up excuses than it would have taken to complete the task in the first place. If you are one of these, then time mastery is not going to be a pleasant experience for you.

We live in a litigious world where everyone blames everyone else for their own fallings. I can sue you after 40 years of smoking because I did not know it was not good for me. How could I not know it was not good for me? One would have had to have lived in a hole at the South Pole not to know that smoking is not good for us.

If we are to achieve great things then we need to take responsibility for everything in our lives, and decide to make the changes necessary in order to live a stress free life and enjoy every moment we are here. After all, we are only here on this planet for a short time, just visiting really, so let us have a ball and make sure what we do adds to the

---

LIFE TIP

Excuses will get you of the hook or out of a tight spot but will never get you where you want to go.

happiness of everyone with whom we come into contact. And when we leave the planet, to make sure it is in at least as good a condition as we found it, for the next visitors.

Its time to now look at bringing all of this together so that we have a working tool to make our own S.M.A.R.T.E.R. Action Plans and compile our daybook task lists right through to a working daily to-do list. Right! Where do we start? As with all things, we must begin with the end in mind so what is it we are trying to achieve?

1.   Desired outcome.
2.   Where am I today, at this moment?
3.   Time scale to achievement.
4.   What are my motivators for this action plan?
5.   Can I take action on these points?
6.   Who else needs to be involved?
7.   Where can I get the information I need?
8.   What format am I going to use?
9.   How am I going to measure it?
10. When am I going to review it?
11. Who can I get to be a mentor for this action plan?

We can add to this list if needed, and you will find that most of the questions should be asked every time we set up an action plan. We then added these points to the S.M.A.R.T.E.R. format, and we're half way home. Let's work through a time related task to see the steps that are necessary to achieve a workable action plan.

S = Stretching

Let's say you need to find an hour extra a day to get to some of the new tasks you want to achieve. Remember, it is not the intention of this book to get you more time in bed, unless this is your biggest problem with time management. We all only need about six to seven hours a night to live long and happy lives which, for most of us, means about eight hours a day in the bedroom getting to sleep, waking up and getting dressed. For a man, say, nine hours; a lady seems to need more time to get ready and though I do not mean this to sound sexist, from experience it appears to be so. This leads me to observe that if we are looking for extra time, this area is always a good place to start.

We have decided that it is first thing in the morning where the problems arise. We set the alarm or opportunity clock for 6a.m. and get out of bed in a bad mood, tired and tense at 8a.m. Do you know how tiring it is to sleep in fifteen minute intervals as we lean out of bed and hit the snooze button for the next seven times that the clock's alarm goes off?

Step one is to begin with the end in mind. One hour is all we need, so let's set the clock for 7a.m., and we only have to hit the snooze button three times now. In achieving this, we will be stretching; we will have achieved something we have not done before.

M = Motivational

Is getting up at 7a.m. a really motivational thing to do? I think not, so let's review our motivators. Where has the need for the extra hour come from? The action plan that you drew up last night, when you had finished you quiet time, centred on your decision to lose some weight, so you are going for a jog each morning and believe that it will need about an hour to get around the course that you have set yourself. So we use the motivators to set this one up. This is a thing people do not generally do; mixing and matching their plans. They find it hard to achieve multiple things, but if we tie them together so that as we complete one part, we have engaged a part of the next motivator.

The civilized man has built a carriage, but has lost the use of his feet. He is supported on crutches, but lacks the support of his muscle. He has a fine Geneva watch, but he fails in the skills to tell the hour by the sun.

Ralph Waldo Emerson

Motivators shape a fitness action plan:

1. Live longer.
2. Lose weight.
3. Look younger.
4. Better choice of clothes.
5. More energy.
6. Sleep better.
7. Be able to see my children and grandchildren grow up.

As you can see, with some plans there are small sub-plans, but as long as they are not too complex, then we are fine.

A = Actionable
Can we take action on these points set out above? Not really.

They are all outcomes in their own right. So we need to include points that are actionable. The best way to tackle this area is to have small points that include action words.

1. I will *do*
2. My new regime is *to...*
3. I *will get up* every morning at 0700 hours
4. On Tuesday I *will...*
5. I am going *to...*
6. This *will* happen.
7. By X I *will be...*
8. I have *achieved* this...
9. My enjoyment *has grown* as my actions have been maintained.
10. I *will use* this time to...

R = Reviewable
This part of the plan is reviewable every day as it is a daily task that we are setting for ourselves. Every day that we achieve, do not

achieve or plan we will know it straight away. To this end, this kind of plan can look very simplistic but that is what we are trying to achieve. It is most important that we decide how and when we are going to record our success or otherwise in this. So we can put this part of our plan into place at the beginning.

- Each morning I will get up at 0700 hours from Tuesday the 5th of next month.
- Week 1 and my alarm clock will be set for 0745. I am going to put it on the chair on the other side of the room so that I will have to get up to turn it off.
- Week 2 and I will set my alarm clock at 0730.
- Week 3 and I will set my alarm clock at 0715.
- Week 4 and I will set my alarm clock at 0700.

From then on I will get up at 0700 hours so that I can achieve my goal of running for one hour per day. I will set out a spreadsheet to record my daily achievement:

As you can see, things started out hard then as we get into the swing

	Monday	Tuesday	Wednesday	Thursday	Friday	Saturday	Sunday
Achieved							
Week 1	08.00hr	07.45hr	07.45hr	08.15hr	07.38hr	09.00hr	07.45hr
Week 2	07.45hr	07.30hr	07.30hr	07.30hr	07.30hr	07.30hr	07.30hr
Week 3	07.15hr	07.15hr	07.15hr	07.15hr	07.15hr	07.45hr	09.00hr
Week 4	07.00hr	07.15hr	07.00hr	07.00hr	07.00hr	09.00hr	08.00hr
Week 5	07.00hr	07.00hr	07.00hr	07.00hr	07.00hr	08.00hr	09.00hr
Week 6	07.00hr	07.00hr	07.00hr	07.00hr	07.00hr	08.30hr	08.30hr
Week 7	07.00hr	07.00hr	07.00hr	07.00hr	07.00hr	08.00hr	08.30hr
Week 8	07.00hr	07.00hr	07.00hr	07.00hr	07.00hr	08.00hr	08.30hr
Week 9	07.00hr	07.00hr	07.00hr	07.00hr	07.00hr	08.00hr	08.30hr

Week 10	07.00hr	07.00hr	07.00hr	07.00hr	07.00hr	08.00hr	08.30hr
Week 11	07.00hr	07.00hr	07.00hr	07.00hr	07.00hr	08.00hr	08.30hr
Week 12	07.00hr	07.00hr	07.00hr	07.00hr	07.00hr	08.00hr	08.30hr
Week 13	07.00hr	07.00hr	07.00hr	07.00hr	07.00hr	08.00hr	08.30hr
Week 14	07.00hr	07.00hr	07.00hr	07.00hr	07.00hr	08.00hr	08.30hr
Week 15	07.00hr	07.00hr	07.00hr	07.00hr	07.00hr	08.00hr	08.30hr

of it all, it became routine. With this simple spreadsheet we can record our times and get an understanding of where we are at any point in our achievement. We should see that by the end of week 9 we are running in accordance with the plan all of the time, and it will be hard to revert back to getting up out of bed later.

You can also see that weekends have changed and we have settled on getting up a bit later as we do not have to go work so we can still have our run before the day starts in earnest.

Very simply, can it be reviewed? Yes! And I can now extend this to most other time-related plans I may have. With the exercise of staging our first four weeks action plan, we have given ourselves the chance to slowly start building up our mastery of time muscles and embed our new routine.

T = Time bound

This plan has some time planning in it but is it time bound? If we look at it, the plan sets out the objective of getting up at 0700 hours to run. We have set out in our plan a lead-time in which to achieve this and we are looking at attaining our objective within four weeks. As we see from our log book, the end result is that we achieved our goal within the time scale set out in this plan but not in the action words so we needed to add these to the final version.

E = Evidenced

Is the plan evidenced? I believe the simple chart is evidence that we did it. Having the chart at the beginning also proves that we had a plan of action and those we were taking steps along the way to record our achievements.

R = Reviewed

However, if we do not maintain our log for long enough we can become blasé and say, ah! Well I get it done most of the time and so we start to drift. One thing that is for certain is that we never drift forward; we always drift backwards. We need to review this plan after six months to see if we can achieve this in an extended period of time and then to maintain our plan once we have achieved it.

If we look at the action plan it would look like the table opposite. As you can see, this is a very simple plan, but it contains all of the main elements. If we then look at the full spreadsheet, it will look as shown on page 100.

We will see that we did not always hit the target set at the beginning, but as we reviewed it at the proper times, we were able to make the small changes that were needed to achieve our long-term goals. This is the key to our success in this type of life changing action plan.

We get better and better at putting these plans in place so that we are then able to set up similar plans for all areas of our lives, giving greater flexibility in our time planning as we release ourselves from the time limiting activities in which we have been engaged. The successful implementation of these plans will also get you to a place in time where you are helping others to make changes to their lives in similar ways; sharing your plans and how you achieved success in your specific areas by overcoming your problems – and believe me, there will be problems.

Action Plan   **Date 01/01/03**

IMPROVE FITNESS AND LOSS WEIGHT

1. Target weight is 12 stone.
2. Target date is the 1st of June 2004.
3. This is 15 months.
4. Current Weight is 18 stone = 6 stone in 18 months.
5. = 4.66 lbs per month.
6. = 1lbs 1 ounce per week.
7. Current time for 4 mile run = 1 hour.
8. Improve time for run to 8 mins per mile by July 2003.
9. Extend run to 5 miles in July and to 6 miles in Dec 2003.

Motivators for fitness action plan

1. Live longer.
2. Lose weight.
3. Look younger.
4. Better choice of clothes.
5. More energy.
6. Sleep better.
7. Be able to see my children grow up.

Action words and activities

1. Run 4 miles per day.
2. Devise diet (separate plan attached).
3. Review of working practice to include proper eating times.
4. Enjoying new, higher energy levels.
5. Wake up every morning at 07.00 hrs (separate plan attached).
6. Review plan weekly, complete weight chart.
7. Play 5 a side every Tuesday.
8. Keep run time log.
9. Review distance run every month, look at extending.
10. Make an appointment with doctor and fitness consultant for health checks and advice.

Best time and distance per month

Jan-03	Feb-03	Mar-03	Apr-03	May-03	Jun-03
4 miles	4 miles	4 miles	4.5 miles	5miles	5miles
62mins	58mins	56mins	56 mins	5mins	43mins
Jul-03	Aug-03	Sep-03	Oct-03	Nov-03	Dec-03
6miles	6miles	6 miles	6miles	6.5 miles	6.5 miles
56min	50mins	48mins	45mines	48mins	46mines
Jan-04	Feb-04	Mar-04	Apr-04	May-04	Jun-04
6.5 miles	7miles	7miles	7.5 miles	8 miles	8 miles
40 mins	56mins	53mins	50 mins	57 mins	54mins
Jul-04					
8 miles					
50 mins					

Daily get up data

	Monday	Tuesday	Wednesday	Thursday	Friday	Saturday	Sunday
Achieved							
Week 1	08.00hr	07.45hr	07.45hr	08.15hr	07.38hr	09.00hr	07.45hr
Week 2	07.45hr	07.30hr	07.30hr	07.30hr	07.30hr	07.30hr	07.30hr
Week 3	07.15hr	07.15hr	07.15hr	07.15hr	07.15hr	07.45hr	09.00hr
Week 4	07.00hr	07.15hr	07.00hr	07.00hr	07.00hr	09.00hr	08.00hr
Week 5	07.00hr	07.00hr	07.00hr	07.00hr	07.00hr	08.00hr	09.00hr
Week 6	07.00hr	07.00hr	07.00hr	07.00hr	07.00hr	08.30hr	08.30hr
Week 7	07.00hr	07.00hr	07.00hr	07.00hr	07.00hr	08.00hr	08.30hr
Week 8	07.00hr	07.00hr	07.00hr	07.00hr	07.00hr	08.00hr	08.30hr
Week 9	07.00hr	07.00hr	07.00hr	07.00hr	07.00hr	08.00hr	08.30hr
Week 10	07.00hr	07.00hr	07.00hr	07.00hr	07.00hr	08.00hr	08.30hr
Week 11	07.00hr	07.00hr	07.00hr	07.00hr	07.00hr	08.00hr	08.30hr
Week 12	07.00hr	07.00hr	07.00hr	07.00hr	07.00hr	08.00hr	08.30hr
Week 13	07.00hr	07.00hr	07.00hr	07.00hr	07.00hr	08.00hr	08.30hr
Week 14	07.00hr	07.00hr	07.00hr	07.00hr	07.00hr	08.00hr	08.30hr
Week 15	07.00hr	07.00hr	07.00hr	07.00hr	07.00hr	08.00hr	08.30hr

Target Weight

	Jan-03	Feb-03	Mar-03	Apr-03	May-03	Jun-03	Jul-03
Week 1	18st 2lbs	17st 12lbs	17st 12lbs	17st 4lbs	16st 11lbs	16st 5lbs	15st 8lbs
Week 2	17st 12lbs	17st 12lbs	17st 8lbs	17st	16st 10lbs	16st 7lbs	15st 7lbs
Week 3	17st 13lbs	17st 11lbs	17st 7lbs	16st 12lbs	16st 9lbs	16st 5lbs	15st 6lbs
Week 4	18st 2lbs	17st 10lbs	17st 5lbs	16st 12lbs	16st 8lbs	16st 3lbs	15st 5lbs

	Aug-03	Sep-03	Oct-03	Nov-03	Dec-03	Jan-04	Feb-04
Week1	15st 4lbs	14st 12lbs	14st 2lbs	13st 11lbs	13st 7lbs	13st 3lbs	12st 12lbs
Week2	15st 3lbs	14st 8lbs	14st 2lbs	13st 10lbs	13st 6lbs	13st 2lbs	12st 10lbs
Week3	15st 2lbs	14st 6lbs	14st 2lbs	13st 9lbs	13st 5lbs	13st 1lbs	12st 10lbs
Week4	15st 1lbs	14st 4lbs	14st	13st 8lbs	13st 4lbs	12st 12lbs	12st 8lbs

	Mar-04	Apr-04	May-04	Jun-04	Jul-04
Week 1	12st 7lbs	12st 3lbs	12st 2lbs	12st 2lbs	12st 2lbs
Week 2	12st 6lbs	12st 3lbs	12st 2lbs	12st 2lbs	12st 2lbs
Week 3	12st 5lbs	12st 3lbs	12st 2lbs	12st 2lbs	12st 2lbs
Week 4	12st 4lbs	12st 3lbs	12st 2lbs	12st 2lbs	12st 2lbs

EIGHTEEN

CONCLUSION

Sacred time is the collapse of the past and future into an eternal nowso that the heroics of our ancestors and our descendants are forever part of the present.
Prof. M. Kearl, *A Sociological Tour through Cyberspace Times Sacred and profane*

Earlier in this book time travel was mentioned, and I said that we would take a look at the subject towards the end of the book, so here we go. If you read books and articles on time travel, the authors will have all sorts of complicated mathematical equations that, due to the way in which the universe is made, ostensibly prove that it is possible to only travel forward. Some will say that both future and past are possible, but you cannot travel back in time as yet because no-one has come up with a time machine. Once a time machine is in existence, they say, it will only be possible to travel back in time as far as the era when the time machine came into working existence. Are you confused yet? Well, let us look at things in a more relevant way.

We all have the ability to move through time whenever we wish. When we are with our parents we travel mentally back in time to when we were younger. This is our mental lock-in date, so that when we are with a person or in a certain house or smell a certain fragrance, we are transported back to that very moment. This happens to us throughout our lives, with each person and every event locked inside our minds forever, and we use these to guide us into the future. For some of us this will be a good thing; for others it may not be very uplifting.

To move into a future that we want is the whole essence of proper time management. If we get this right, then all things that we are planning to have will come to us when we need them to. Planning the future is very important as we have the ability to create our own future realities today and then work on them so that we not only have the life we wished for and imagined, but the time to enjoy it. If you have read this far then you will have many working ideas by now on how to achieve better and more effective time management. Combined with a positive forward planning diary, these working ideas will give you the impetus to get things moving forward. I believe that once we have time under control we can then move on to the next stage.

In the next book in this series we will explore that stage, and explain why it is so crucial. Is leaving the rat race by joining it, the real and ordered step that we must take to truly take control of our own lives?

We will explore the exodus from the UK that is now taking place, and its reflection of the quest to seek a lifestyle that from a distance appears idyllic. As we know, in today's world things are moving at an ever-increasing rate. Work and home life seem to be diametrically opposed, and the result is a population where obesity, illness, the breakdown of the family unit, unhappiness and a deeper dependency on recreational drugs, alcohol and reality TV are our new realities. They are realities that are leaving us catatonic and seemingly impervious to all human suffering.

Intolerance is on the increase; new phenomena such as road rage and the re-emergence of the religious tensions of past centuries are again on the rise. However, things are never as bad as they appear to be portrayed by the media and with some degree of reflection, thought and a sense of purpose and proportion, life can again become a pleasure for us. In taking on these new realities, we discover that joining in can effect a reduction in stress that equates and perhaps can surpass the relief gained by departure.

Explore your own abilities and talents. Look at what it is you are working towards and understand the right way to achieve it. There is a simple process on how to make a contract with your boss or company; profit and pleasure for all concerned can be the result.

This book has given you the practical guidance to find the right balance between work and your life. Join the team and start your own group of 'escapees' to achieve King Rat status and start living the life you thought you had. Explore the power of the four segments and the contract you have made with each and every objective that is important to you – and you will never look back.

**The Life you always wanted but thought you were
not entitled to be that happy, starts today –
and never look back.**